PATHS IN SP

*Also by John Macquarrie and
published by SCM Press*

Christian Unity and Christian Diversity
The Faith of the People of God
God-Talk
The Humility of God
Principles of Christian Theology
Thinking about God
Twentieth-Century Religious Thought
A Dictionary of Christian Ethics (ed)

Paths in Spirituality

JOHN MACQUARRIE

SCM PRESS LTD

334 01243 0

First published 1972
by SCM Press Ltd
26–30 Tottenham Road, London N1 4BZ
Second edition 1992

Printed in Great Britain by
Mackays of Chatham, Kent

Contents

TO FATHER GARFIELD

Preface to the Second Edition

For many years I have been writing on the subject of Christianity, but this book is different from most of the others I have written. These other books were in the main theological and dealt with intellectual problems in Christian faith, especially with the central problem of how, in our late twentieth-century science-oriented culture, it is possible to continue to believe with integrity in God, in Jesus Christ and in a hopeful destiny for the human race. The present book, though it does not forsake theology, is more concerned with the *practice* of religion than with the problems of *belief*. By the 'practice' of religion, I mean prayer, worship, contemplation – the whole range of doing and experiencing that falls under the vaguely defined term 'spirituality'.

The first edition of the book appeared about twenty years ago, when there was something like a crisis of spirituality. In Europe and North America, the majority of people, even though they remained nominally Christians and professed a general though somewhat hazy allegiance to 'Christian values', had abandoned regular worship and prayer. It was fashionable among some preachers to expound 'secular' or 'religionless' Christianity, though such language could mean many things and could be affirmative as well as negative. It was in that situation that I felt that I had to swim against the current, and defend some of the practices that were in danger of being swept away.

Of course, there were many others who felt much as I did. The Sociologist Peter Berger was expressing the belief that when secularism has reached its extreme development, people will turn away in dissatisfaction. As if in confirmation of this belief, many young people were searching for a spiritual goal beyond those offered by the consumer society. Liturgical reformers were seeking with mixed success to find more vital and meaningful modes of worship. Even so, in spite of some hopeful

signs of renewal, there has not been much change in the twenty
years since this book first appeared. I still feel that I am swim-
ming against the current, and that many readers will think that
what is commended in these pages is out of date. But if it
encourages some people to seek communion with God, perhaps
even to find it, it will be worthwhile.

Inevitably, a book such as this cannot be entirely free of
autobiography and personal preference. Therefore I have commended those forms of prayer and worship which have meant
most to me in my own history. This means in fact that I have
stressed the sacramental approach to God. But I have freely
acknowledged that there are many paths of spirituality other
than those commended here.

In this revised and enlarged edition of the book, some of the
earlier parts have been rewritten, partly to make the language
more 'inclusive', partly to take account of some liturgical
changes of recent years. Three new chapters have been added.
Chapter IX, 'Eucharistic Sacrifice', had its origin in an address
given at Baltimore Cathedral in 1987, at a celebration recognizing the contribution of Fr Donald Garfield to the new American
Book of Common Prayer. Chapter XIII, 'The Reconciliation
of a Penitent', was written as a discussion document at the
request of the General Synod of the Church of England and
published by the Synod as a pamphlet in 1987. Chapter XIV,
'Rest and Restlessness in Christian Spirituality', was written as
my contribution to the *Festschrift* for the late Canon Edward N.
West of the Cathedral of St John the Divine, New York: *Spirit
and Light*, ed. William B. Green and Madeleine L. Engle (Seabury Press 1976). I express my thanks to those concerned for
permission to publish this material here.

Oxford   John Macquarrie
July 1992

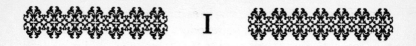

The Practice of Religion

This book deals with the themes of worship, prayer and spirituality. The nature of these activities, some of the forms which they take and the value to be assigned to them will be explored in subsequent chapters. For the moment, it may be enough to say that they all have to do with the practice of religion, and I have to begin by acknowledging that nowadays this has become problematical. Among many people, the ideal of the saint, the person who has become proficient in the practice of religion, is no longer an appealing one. Christianity is still prized by many for the sake of its ethical teachings or because of the impressive figure of Jesus Christ, but its definitely religious side, worship, prayer and the rest, is frequently regarded with some suspicion even by people within the Church.

We have indeed in recent years heard the expression 'religion-less Christianity'. While this has had no single meaning among those who have advocated it, it has always implied the de-emphasizing of worship, prayer and the spiritual life, and its champions have urged that our energies should instead be channelled into the practical applications of Christianity in personal and social relations. Some of them have told us that we have entered an age when men have outgrown religion. They say that insistence on the religious dimension of Christianity has become a barrier which prevents secular men from committing themselves to the Christian life style. In the eyes of such critics, the practice of religion has become an embarrassment, and a hindrance to the veritable Christian mission.

But religion is refusing to die. I am referring not merely to the fact that many theologians have remained unconvinced that a secularized or religionless Christianity is an adequate version of the Gospel or that it responds to the full range of contemporary needs. More important is the evidence afforded by the remarkable upsurge of religion (or religiosity) among young people, especially in the United States, that most secularized and technologically advanced of all countries. Many of the young people there have become disenchanted with the values of a secular culture and have sought to build up a 'counter culture'[1] in which, as they believe, they will be able to develop as persons in a fuller way than is now open to them. A religious dimension is a normal constituent of the counter culture. Admittedly, much of the religiosity of the counter culture has been quite non-Christian, and has expressed itself in explorations into Eastern mysticism, the psychodelic and the occult. As Carl Braaten has shrewdly observed, instead of getting 'Christianity without religion', we have witnessed 'the revival of religion without Christianity'.[2] Where the new religiosity has flowed in Christian channels, it has found expression in revivalist and Pentecostalist sects rather than in the staid mainline denominations.[3] This may be partly because these denominations seem in the eyes of the youth to be closely associated with the prevailing bourgeois culture, and partly because worship and liturgy have become so trivialized in most American churches that those in search of a spirituality have thought it necessary to look elsewhere.

Let me confess that I view these new upsurges of religious experience with mixed feelings. I am not surprised by the continuing vitality of religion. Its demise has often been predicted, but it has not happened and is not likely to happen. I believe (and later I shall seek to show) that our humanity has a religious dimension and cannot be fulfilled where this is denied or neglected. Even if the specific forms of these new religious movements should prove ephemeral, they point to a continuing demand for religious fulfilment. Experiences of the death of God, the loss of the sense of the holy, the demise of religion are characteristic of an affluent bourgeois society, and the young, or some of them, are in protest against such a society because they believe that it diminishes their humanity and hinders their development as persons. It is interesting to note that black Americans take the same view, and several black theologians have indicated that the 'death of God' is a phenomenon of the white middle class and has nothing to do with the black experience. For instance, J. Deotis Roberts tells us: 'Blacks, of all people, are instinctively religious.' He also says that 'few blacks have been afforded the luxury of disbelieving in the divine existence.'[4] But would we have to suppose that when American blacks – and similar remarks would apply to third world peoples – have all the opportunities of secular affluent society opened to them, they too will forsake their religiousness? It is possible that this may happen, but there are many blacks and third world people determined that they will not have imposed upon them the consumer mentality and the hard unspirituality that have become so dominant in the West. The Brazilian Rubem Alves writes: 'Technology creates a false man, a man who learns how to find happiness in what is given to him by the system. His soul is created as the image of what he can have.'[5] Alves – and others who share his point of view – is more interested in men as bearers of freedom and dignity than as consumers of goods. I believe that the practice of religion, properly understood, is an important dimension of human freedom and dignity, though it is neglected or even rejected by that consumer mentality which is so widespread in the secularized societies of the West. The advocates of secular Christianity were surely themselves affected by the dominant outlook of affluent consumer societies. Though I have never denied that they have had some genuine insights, I have never been able to go along with them, not merely on account of the onesidedness of their theology but even more because of the hard unspirituality which has characterized many of the expressions of their position. It is only fair to add, however, that some of the leaders of the secular style of theology have changed their minds about the place of religion and now set a much higher valuation upon it. Harvey Cox is an interesting exemplar of this new appreciation for religion. He writes: 'Man is more essentially religious than many of us have assumed. He thirsts for mystery, meaning, community and even for some sort of ritual.'[6]

But I have admitted that I regard the revival of religion with mixed feelings. I welcome it, to the extent that it means that contemporary man is not going to permit his nature to be truncated by the excision of the religious dimension. Yet I am uneasy about the uncritical character of the new religiousness and the ease with which people seem able to forget the more salutary truths which were seeking expression in the secular theologies. For the critique of religion advanced by secular theology, though far too sweeping and exaggerated, did have a measure of validity. It was simply the continuation of a critique which began in ancient times in both Israel and Greece, and has been developed in modern times by Feuerbach, Marx, Nietzsche, Freud and many others. Anyone who has been a pastor is bound to acknowledge that much religion fails to stand up to this critique. The practice of religion has been and still is linked with evils and weaknesses of one kind or another – with ignorance, superstition, opposition to science; with a false other-worldliness that leads to indifference in the face of social injustice; with immaturity and the refusal to grow up and to accept responsibility; with fanaticisms that have stood in the way of friendship and co-operation; with a self-centred, inward-looking quest for salvation. Like many other powerful factors in human life – technology, for instance – religion can lead to bad results as well as good. It can diminish our humanity as well as enhance it. Thus, when one hears of upsurges of religious experience like those mentioned above, one cannot help feeling some malaise, especially as much of the new religiosity seems to be almost entirely void of any intellectual content. Is the exuberant spirit of celebration as onesided as the drab secularity which has provoked it? If so, it could turn out to be very dangerous.

The only worship, prayer and spirituality, the only practice of religion I shall defend will be of the kind that has been rigorously subjected to the critique of religion, and I shall keep coming back to the critical questions throughout this book. Yet I believe that the practice of religion, when purged of egoism, brought to maturity, related to real life, encompassing intellect as well as emotion and will, makes an indispensable contribution toward the development of a fully human person.

Humanity has a religious dimension which cannot be either suppressed or annexed to some other dimension of human existence, such as the moral or the aesthetic. This religious dimension is not easily described. We might call it 'communion with God', but this is an expression which would itself call for eludication and which we cannot use to beg the question. Persons in whom the religious dimension has been brought to a high level of development are called saints. They are not only good but holy as well, and their holiness does not seem to be just another moral quality. Perhaps it is not to be found apart from moral qualities, but it is itself not an additional quality but rather an accompaniment of all the others. We might describe it as an inner strength or an inner depth, at once stable and dynamic. It has also a creative character – saints are not only good, they enable others to be good, just by the kind of person they are. The inner strength welling up in them overflows in their relations with others.

Saints are rare, but we all meet persons who, in greater or less degree, have something of the religious dimension. Such a person has developed this through prayer, worship and spiritual discipline, and has taken at least a few steps along that road, the goal of which is sainthood. H. H. Price has well described the kind of individual we have in mind: 'A spiritual person feels himself to be "more at home" in the universe than unspiritual persons do. He has a certain serenity and inward peace which others cannot help envying and even admiring.' Price goes on to say that 'The existence of such persons is in practice the most persuasive argument in favour of a religious world-outlook, and probably always has been.'[7]

It is interesting that this description of the spiritual person and the high evaluation of his qualities should come from a philosopher, and interesting too that he should say these qualities excite envy and admiration among those who are without them. This may not always be the case, but I believe that it often is. Now, these qualities could scarcely be admired or even understood unless there were some latent capacity or tendency for their development in those who are without them. My thesis is that a fully human, fully personal being is one in whom the religious dimension has been developed, and that the capacity for religion belongs to all of us. This is borne out by the fact that even among non-religious persons we find modes of experience and even spiritual practices which are analogous to, or inchoate versions of, the definitely religious forms of spirituality. This explains too the fact that some non-religious persons occasionally exhibit something of that serenity and inward peace which

Price rightly mentions as specially characteristic of those committed to a religious world-outlook. Religionlessness cannot be
simply equated with what I have called 'hard unspirituality'.
At various points in this book I shall draw attention to parallels
between specifically Christian practices and related modes of
secular experience, for while I have said – as Price also says –
that the religious dimension cannot be subsumed under the
moral, this does not mean that it is something utterly isolated.
On the contrary, it is a natural human development, like, say,
the aesthetic sense. Its roots are there, waiting to be nourished
into growth. Yet, again like the aesthetic sense, it can be left
neglected and then it may wither away. As Michael Novak has
remarked, 'The religious sense is a sense that needs effort,
practice and exploration, like any other.'[8] We do indeed speak
of grace and of the divine initiative, but these ideas must not be
made the excuse for spiritual sloth. Proficiency in the practice
of religion demands that we should make the appropriate effort
and application.

So I am claiming that man, even twentieth-century man,
needs the practice of religion for the fulfilment of his humanity.
As Teilhard de Chardin has expressed it, 'The more man
becomes man, the more will he become prey to a need, a need
that is always more explicit, more subtle and more magnificent,
the need to adore.'[9] Is this a false reading of the situation? Does
the truth lie rather with those who say that the capacity for
religion, and especially for worship and adoration, has dried up
in contemporary man and that in any case these things are no
longer needed? Partly, it will depend on what we mean by
worship and adoration, and on whether the critique of religion
has been heeded and its lessons learned. Let us recall Teilhard's
words that the need to adore is one that becomes 'more explicit,
more subtle and more magnificent'. If we in our time are to
experience the need to adore, then adoration will need to be
interpreted more subtly than on the model of homage paid to
an absolute monarch, which is how many people do think of it,
and they can scarcely do otherwise in view of so much of the
traditional language. But 'to adore' (Latin: *ad-orare*) is 'to pray
toward . . .' It is to go out of oneself, to commune with a
Reality larger, deeper, purer than one's own being. Adoration is
an enhancement of one's being, though paradoxically this comes

about through going out of oneself. To return for a moment to
Teilhard, we find him expressing it thus: 'To adore . . . that
means to lose oneself in the unfathomable, to plunge into the
inexhaustible, to find peace in the incorruptible, to be absorbed
in defined immensity, to offer oneself to the fire and the trans-
parency, to annihilate oneself as one becomes more deliberately
conscious of oneself, and to give of one's deepest to that whose
depth has no end.'[10]

Let me now set forth a few guidelines which may point the
direction in which we can look for a renewed spirituality. In
these guidelines we shall take account of the critique of religion
and prepare the way for the discussions of prayer, worship and
spirituality which lie ahead.

1. We must keep in view the fulfilling character of the practice of religion, as aiming at a fuller personal being for man.
God is not glorified through the denigration of man or by having
man abased before him. On the contrary, he is glorified as man
attains a being more nearly conformed to the image of God.
Feuerbach once said that in the teaching of Luther, God is
everything, man nothing. 'God is virtue, beauty, sweetness,
power, health, amiability; man is personified depravity, con-
trariness, hatefulness, worthlessness and uselessness. Luther's
doctrine is divine but inhuman, indeed, barbaric – a hymn to
God but a lampoon of man.'[11] One could use almost the same
words about much traditional worship. Certainly, there is a
place for penitence and humility. But if worship is to fulfil our
humanity, it must bring man into his dignity as a spiritual
creature. It must be liberating and enhancing.

2. Closely related to our first point is a second, namely, that
if worship is to be understood as fulfilling, then its eschatological
significance must be stressed. Many people are familiar with
Eliade's theory of the religious act as the repetition of a divine
archetype. Much worship is in fact understood as the continuation of a pattern of behaviour in a community and the
maintenance of the values of that community. This is indeed
true and important and represents the stabilizing effect of
worship. But worship is also an attempt to experience even now
the end that lies ahead. Its dynamic role is to bring heaven into
the present. This is well illustrated in the Christian Eucharist,
which is both a memorial or *anamnesis* of Christ's saving work

and an anticipation of the heavenly banquet. If worship is to be fulfilling, dynamic and creative, then its eschatological reference will need to be stressed more than it has been.

3. Mention of heaven in the last paragraph must not be misunderstood. The critique of religion has rightly pointed to the fact that prayer and worship have often been a way of escape from the real world. A contemporary spirituality, while indeed it must be forward looking, must also be closely related to the world in which our lives are set. This is no new problem, and it has always been recognized that the practice of religion is little more than hypocrisy unless it issues in action in human affairs. Schleiermacher considered it 'self-evident to every Christian that prayer necessarily includes and presupposes personal activity in bringing about what is prayed for', but he was wise enough to understand that action without prayer is, from a Christian point of view, just as much a failure as prayer without action.[12] It is easier to diagnose this problem than to solve it, but it seems to me that the long continued stress on the monarchy and transcendence of God, and the type of spirituality associated with it, have tended to separate religion from our tasks in the world, and that a recovery of the doctrine of the immanence of God is needed. However, one must also guard against the idea that every act of prayer or worship should be seen to have a cash-value, so to speak – this is the consumer mentality again.

4. A last point concerns the relation of the individual and corporate aspects of spirituality. To many people, the very word 'spirituality' is associated with the striving for individual salvation. The spiritual man is equated with the 'pietist', and this has become a bad word nowadays, designating the man who is so concerned with the cultivation of his inner life that he is blind to the social and political realities around him. (Whether historically the word 'pietist' has deserved to be devalued in this way is at least debatable.) Certainly any contemporary spirituality must break out from merely individual limits and have its corporate aspect. But the problem of a truly spiritual community is possibly the most difficult of all.

If worship, prayer and spirituality are to be purged of the weaknesses exposed by the critique of religion and are, in strengthened and renewed form, to make their unique contribution to the upbuilding of a truly human and personal existence, then we have to try to understand them in new ways. Yet I believe that in the Christian heritage, and especially the eucharistic heritage, there is a vast treasury of untapped resources, latent emphases and flexible forms on which we can draw for our contemporary spiritual needs.

In the first half of this book (up to the end of Chapter VI) I shall explore in more detail the meaning of worship, prayer and spirituality. In the second half I shall be mainly concerned with interpreting the particular forms which I have found most helpful in my own experience, for an autobiographical element seems to be inevitable in a book of this kind. But while I hope that some of my readers will be attracted to the paths in spirituality which I describe, I am well aware that there is no one road in these matters, and I hope that some readers will be stimulated to explore other ways.

Faith, Worship, Life

The Christian religion is a unity within which all its different parts and modes of expression belong together. These several parts can only be understood and appreciated in the context of the whole, and if we allow any one of them to be isolated, it soon becomes distorted and it may wither away and die. The unity, so the Christian believes, is founded on the unity of God's action – an action on the whole personal being of man within the community of faith. God's action and God's claim are upon the whole, and the only worthy response is one that is made by the whole man.

Of course, our minds are limited in what they can grasp at any one time, and it is characteristic of human life that at any particular moment there is one main thing that occupies our attention. We cannot grasp the whole meaning of the Christian religion all at once, or simultaneously respond to all the ways in which it impinges upon us. Its meaning is inexhaustible and its impact upon us greater than we ever consciously realize. In actual experience, there is always some aspect or some demand of the Christian reality that stands out and occupies the disciple's attention. Yet, whatever this may be, it has also to be related to the whole fabric.

For instance, it may be that some particular doctrine is occupying our attention, let us say, the doctrine of the Church. The more we reflect on this doctrine, the more we recognize that it is inseparable from others – from the doctrines of creation, incarnation, reconciliation, in a word, the whole inexhaustible mystery of the God who has drawn near in Jesus Christ. But even when we have placed the particular doctrine within a wider theological framework, we realize that we are still dealing with an abstraction and are far from the whole. Theology itself, as the intellectual clarification and interpretation of faith, cannot be isolated from the whole life of faith. Theology makes sense only in the context of worship and action.

There are three major factors combined together in the living unity of the Christian religion: doctrine, worship and deeds. I am reminded of a saying in the Old Testament: 'A threefold cord is not quickly broken.'[1] The strength of the Christian religion lies in this complex texture embracing the whole of human life. The three factors are intertwined, so that each strengthens the other. Together they form something that can stand up to the greatest strains without giving way. But if we allow the strands to become separated, then any one of them in isolation begins to show weaknesses and will not maintain itself for long.

Perhaps in the past the commonest error was to isolate doctrine. Faith was understood as belief or intellectual assent. Christians were judged by their orthodoxy, that is to say, by the correctness of their beliefs. The Church often tended to give the impression that right doctrine is all that matters and its theology has frequently been of an abstract academic kind, delighting in fine distinctions and speculative ideas, but often far removed from the concrete problems of the Church and the world.

As a theologian, I am myself very much persuaded of the importance of doctrine and of the need to think out the meaning of Christian faith. But, as has already been indicated, theology has to be related to the whole life of the Church. Theology is God-language and, as Wittgenstein expressed it, 'the speaking of language is part of an activity, or of a form of life.'[2] Theology is not an intellectual game that can be pursued on its own, but part of a much bigger whole. The very revelation on which Christian theology founds itself was not originally a set of propositions but the concrete living and dying and rising of Jesus Christ. And so today that revelation can never be captured in sentences, in doctrinal statements, in books of theology. These have their place, but only as parts of something greater still, which they help to interpret. If we have not sadly reduced and neutralized it, the revelation of God will overflow our doctrinal formulas into life and action. These too are revelation. In the fine words of Gabriel Moran, 'Every act formed by charity is a revelation of God. Every word of truth and love, every hand extended in kindness, echoes the inner life of the Trinity.'[3]

The classic criticism of a faith, doctrine or theology which has been allowed to become abstract and isolated from the living reality of the Christian religion was already given in the New Testament: 'You believe that God is one; you do well. Even the demons believe – and shudder.'[4] A faith that does not go beyond intellectual assent is weak or even dead, and certainly falls far short of that living faith where belief is joined with love and service. Could it be that if people nowadays have difficulty in believing in God, this is partly because such a belief has so often been taught in isolation as an abstract intellectual truth?

More recently, however, the pendulum has swung the other way. We have entered on an age of activism and all the stress has been on *doing*. We have been urged to take our religion out into the streets and the marketplace. Along with this activist spirit, there often goes a depreciation of theology and even an indifference to the most fundamental beliefs of the Church. It is suggested that it does not much matter what one believes. All that is necessary is to love the neighbour and to seek to realize the kingdom of God.

No one can deny that there is much justification for these attempts to set the Church to work and to overcome the inertia of a merely conventional religion. The danger arises only when those who summon us to action feel that they need to decry other factors that may be just as important in the total texture of the Christian commitment. Just as faith without works is a sorry caricature of Christianity, so is action that is not rooted in intelligent belief and understanding. The summons to love the neighbour remains ambiguous and imprecise until we know what love is. There are many kinds of love, and the word 'love' is a much abused one. Only through study of the New Testament and its interpretation in the Church – in other words, only through theology – can we learn to discriminate Christian love from some of its easy substitutes. Again, to talk of the kingdom of God is to use empty rhetoric unless this concept has been explored in its biblical and theological significance, and we have grasped something of its transcendent character.

Christian action in the world will not be sustained or carried out in an intelligent and effective manner unless it is supported by doctrinal convictions that have achieved some degree of clarity. This has in fact been clearly recognized by many of the most able and dedicated Christian activists. Walter Rauschenbusch ranks as one of the most outstanding representatives of the Social Gospel in the United States, and it is worth recalling that he wrote: 'We have a social gospel. We need a systematic theology large enough to match it and vital enough to back it.'[5] For him, it could not be a case of choosing one at the expense of the other, for he saw that they need each other and that it is only when they are woven together that they are strong and alive. 'The social gospel needs a theology to make it effective; but theology needs the social gospel to vitalize it.'[6]

I have said something about faith and life, but so far nothing about the remaining strand in the threefold cord, worship. Does it too supply its measure of strength, or has it become totally obsolete in the modern world? In many countries, few people attend public worship any more. It is tolerated as the eccentricity of a minority, and occasionally criticized as a luxury which takes up time and resources that would be better employed in the service of mankind. If the activist is sometimes impatient of theology, he is likely to be just as impatient of worship, or even more so. For although he may become persuaded that he needs some intellectual basis for his action and seeks this basis in theology, the claim of worship is less obvious.

No doubt worship, like doctrine and action, can become isolated, and then it deserves to be criticized, for it is a mere playing at church. But when worship is placed firmly in the context of the whole Christian reality, we soon learn that it is indispensable. It could even be claimed that it is the middle strand of the three and that it holds faith and action together. How does one go from doctrine to action? What holds together the conviction that the inner life of the Trinity is love with the loving deed? Worship does this, for worship is both thought (contemplation) and service (liturgy). Modern criticism of worship will not lead us to abandon it, but it does force us to seek a fuller understanding and a more penetrating explanation of what Christian worship is all about. But we must be careful not to create needless difficulties for ourselves, or set up needless oppositions where in fact there are none. Thus any valid understanding of worship can be attained only by viewing it in the context of the whole Christian religion and by constantly relating it to faith on the one hand and to action on the other. Worship is not some separate activity, but is continuous with the whole of life. Elsewhere I have described worship as 'concentration'[7] – the recollecting or gathering together of the self in a focal moment of encounter with that which is most real and most compelling. This is also to be understood as a creative centre, formative for even the peripheral areas of life.

For the Christian, the worshipful encounter is between man on the one hand and God in Christ on the other. Thus we can think of worship differently as we look at it from one side or the other. We can think of worship as offered to God for the glory of God, or we can think of it as the impact of God's presence on man, pervading and transforming human life. The two sides are complementary and must not be separated, or we would fall again into a false opposition. Neither way of understanding worship makes sense without the other. We do not worship God as if we were offering some kind of external tribute that could somehow please him or increase him – that is the unworthy monarchical model of God and brings worship into disrepute. But we cannot say either that our worship makes no difference to God. He has set us in this world as free and responsible beings and he asks for our co-working in building up his creation in love and righteousness. Hence our worship is for the glory of God to the extent that it is also a transforming of ourselves into God's co-workers.

Pointing out that the Constitution on Sacred Liturgy put out by Vatican II states that 'the liturgy is for the sanctification of man and for the glorification of God', Godfrey Diekman has commented: 'To the degree that in the liturgical action personal faith is quickened and love deepened, to that degree is God glorified . . . What else can be truly worthy of God except persons who believe more fully, who love God and their fellow men more deeply, and learn to do so in the Eucharist?'[8] The glorification of God and the sanctification of man are not competing motives in worship. Indeed, to remember that God is glorified to the extent that man is sanctified is not to detract from the reality of a God-directed worship, but to acknowledge the absolute priority of God in worship. For worship, after all, is not primarily something that we do. It is response to what God has already done and is still doing. It is because God has first of all made us in his own image that we find implanted in us the desire to worship him and to grow in likeness to him. It is God's Spirit working in us that first brings us to worship the mystery of Holy Being and to seek God's grace. The intimate relation of the Godward and manward aspects of worship was well expressed in famous words of St Irenaeus: 'The glory of God is a living man; and the life of man consists in beholding God.'[9]

It is at this point that we may remind ourselves of the power and influence of worship by considering the destructive effects of idolatry in human life. Again there is the reciprocal relation. In idolatry, some finite object has usurped the place of God in man's allegiance. In a strange and sinister way that we rightly call 'demonic', the idol exerts upon human life that overwhelming fascination which is a perverted form of God's attraction for man. The idol establishes for itself a formative centre which begins to shape the life of its worshipper in its own demonic image, so drawing him away from that image of God in which he was created and into which he was destined to grow ever more fully.

If we begin our discussion with the manward aspect of worship, with the effects which it brings about in the lives of the worshippers, it will be understood that it is not being treated in a utilitarian way, as if worship were to be prized only for its practical consequences; and still less am I suggesting that worship is exhausted in its meaning by a psychological interpretation, as if it were to be considered chiefly as a therapeutic exercise. We are proceeding on the assumption that God is really glorified in the sanctification of man, and that the absolute priority in all worship belongs to God.

In its manward aspect, worship (both the public liturgy and supplementary acts of devotion) presents itself as a discipline. The word 'discipline' nowadays is usually associated with harsh methods of training enforced by punishment. But the word means simply 'learning'. Normally, important changes do not take place suddenly in human life. They take time, and the more fundamental they are, the longer time they take. The Christian life, with its demand for self-giving love and for continual growth in likeness to Christ, lays a fundamental and extremely difficult demand upon those who embark upon it. Saints who have spent a lifetime in learning, growing and developing, still bemoan their lack of proficiency in following the Christian way. It is true that we hear of sudden conversions, but we usually find that these have been preparing over a considerable time in the minds of the people concerned; and, more than this, such people do not attain to complete and mature Christian character the moment after conversion.

There are no short cuts from faith (the conviction that Christ is Lord and his love sovereign) to life (the acting out of this faith in daily deeds of self-giving love). On the contrary, this is for most people a long and arduous way. All kinds of obstructions have to be surmounted. There are unloving passions, which may be difficult to control. There are self-regarding and self-indulgent habits, sometimes built up over years and firmly entrenched. Even if we begin to overcome these obstacles, there is a long way to go before we begin to grasp in an affirmative sense the amazing height and breadth and length and depth of the love to which Christians are called. Worship, both in its corporate exercise and in whatever other acts may be appropriate to each individual, is the discipline leading from faith to action. It is the process by which the disciple is formed and becomes increasingly mature in the Christian religion.

St Paul is one of the earliest and best guides on these matters, a true spiritual counsellor. He himself underwent one of the most dramatic conversion experiences in all Christian history. But it seems that the first thing he did after his conversion was to retire for a time to the deserts of Arabia – he went on retreat, as we would say nowadays. He let three years pass before he went up to Jerusalem, and who can doubt that this time was spent in prayer and preparation for the tasks to which he believed himself called by God?[10]

In one of his letters[11] he compares himself to an athlete who has to run in a race. The athlete 'exercises self-control in all things', that is to say, he takes a course of training so that he will be able to run efficiently in the race. The Greek word for such training was *askesis*, and it is interesting to note that the same word could be used for a 'mode of life', for any kind of training does indeed pass over into a life style. As in the case of the word 'discipline', so the English word 'ascetic' has narrowed the meaning to one particular kind of life style, the one character-ized by extreme renunciation and self-mortification. The broader meaning of the original survives in the expression 'ascetical theology' for that branch of theology which deals with the Christian life and its development toward 'mature manhood, to the measure of the stature of the fulness of Christ'.[12]

In one of his fullest and clearest statements[13] on this subject of a training or discipline, Paul contrasts what he calls the 'works of the flesh' with the 'fruits of the Spirit'. The works of the flesh – he mentions, among others, impurity, envy, jealousy, selfishness – are the barriers to the Christian life, indeed, to any decent human existence. Yet they seem to come naturally to us. They have been rife in human society at all times, and they are in evidence today. Only so far as these can be overcome can there be growth toward that other set of qualities Paul mentions – qualities such as love, joy, peace, patience, kindness, goodness, faithfulness, gentleness, self-control. But he calls these 'fruits of the Spirit', for they are to be learned by that immersion in God which we call worship and which allows God's Spirit to operate in human lives and to transform them, replacing the works of the flesh by his own fruits. Paul enunciates a kind of law: 'Whatever a man sows, that he will also reap.' This surely brings us close to the meaning of worship, considered in its manward aspect as a discipline. The communing with God in Christ is like a sowing. It is part of the process of maturing, in which sinful tendencies are weakened and uprooted while the fruits of the Spirit manifest themselves more and more, not only to the benefit of man but to the glory of God.

This is the work of God, the *opus Dei*, in St Benedict's phrase. True worship is work, though one might hardly think this if one has in mind the conventional worship of many Christian churches. It is, furthermore, work which issues in the most valuable results. Again, this will seem an odd claim in a society with a consumer mentality. To people with that mentality, worship and prayer are a waste of time. To be sure, this is not *productive* work, as the economist understands it. It is not work that adds anything to the gross national product. But, more

importantly, it is *creative* work. It is creating persons of spiritual
depth, and through them the creative Spirit will reach out
further still.

Those who think of work as the production of tangible goods
destined for consumption have always been critical of the life of
the religious orders in which some men and women have made
the worship of God the major concern of their lives. But worship
is a work leading to intangible results of the highest value for the
quality of human life, and it is to be hoped that there will
always be some people who, not for themselves alone but for the
whole Church and for all mankind, will devote themselves to
the *opus Dei*. It is possible that we may even see a great revival
of the religious life, for now that industry is becoming increasingly cybernated and automated, some economists are telling us
that the need for persons to be employed on economically productive work will grow less and that there will be a great increase
of leisure time, so that people will be freed for other things. To
be sure, this may not happen as quickly as some have suggested,
and it will happen unevenly in different countries. But as people
are freed from toil, must we not hope that the healing and
fulfilling work of worship will draw many? Already in the
strange phenomena of the hippie communities and of the
counter culture and in the religiosity of many of the young
people we see something like an attempt to rediscover the
religious life. The parallels with the early Franciscans have not
gone unnoticed. Again the search is among young people from
the affluent strata of society. They have found that the gospel of
wealth is not fulfilling and are groping toward contemplation,
perhaps even toward prayer and adoration. But what many of
the contemporary questers seem so far to lack is that structured
discipline or *askesis* which, in various forms, has been worked
out in the Christian tradition. Some also fail to see that true
contemplation cannot be a luxury or an escape for a favoured
élite, but must be a transforming force in the individual and in
society. But we have acknowledged that the Church itself has
been slow to understand that mission and worship are interdependent and each ceases to be meaningful apart from the
other. However, the very emergence of these religious and
quasi-religious stirrings in our time shows us that the ancient
forces still work in human life. Where a dimension of a fully

human life has been cut off, an uneasiness remains and a search begins. This has happened in the case of worship.

But we now return to St Paul and his teaching about the need for a spiritual discipline. We have seen that only as the work of sowing goes on can the fruits of the Spirit be brought to maturity, both in the individual Christian and in society. But Paul wisely recognized that there is no one discipline that can be imposed on all. Indeed, a spiritual discipline cannot be imposed at all. It must be inwardly accepted. But one person differs from another, and the discipline that one finds helpful may not be helpful to someone of a different temperament. In the matter of worship, for instance, I do not suppose that a time will ever come when all Christians will find a single liturgy which will be fulfilling for them all. There ought to be a rich diversity to take care of the wide range of different human needs. This applies not only to worship but to whatever else enters into a Christian life style. We need not all do the same things, though out of the differences one may hope that a harmonious whole can grow up.

Paul's discussion of these matters has arisen out of his teaching about the freedom of the Christian in Christ, and his delivery from enslavement. The law can be for us something external, laid on us in an impersonal way, and this is the kind of slavery which the Christian has left behind. (Unfortunately it is a slavery which the Church has sometimes reimposed by its imposition of an abstract legalistic discipline in worship or in other matters.) The law of Christ is, by contrast, an inward personal discipline. It is not externally imposed but arises from the Christian's incorporation into Christ. It is therefore experienced in terms appropriate to the life of the particular person concerned. Each one 'will have to bear his own load' and is bidden 'to test his own work'.[14] Each one has his own particular weaknesses and areas of life that need strengthening. Equally, each one has his own gifts and his own contributions to make. Each again has his own particular psychological make-up; he learns differently and appropriates differently.

Paul's recognition of the differences makes it plain that there can be no single form of worship or rule of life applicable to all. The European rulers of the sixteenth and seventeenth centuries tried to suppress religious differences and to impose uniformity. Some contemporary ecumenists make the same mistake. But

people refuse to fit preconceived patterns. Yet Paul is not therefore saying it is all a matter of indifference or that no rule is
needed at all. He is treating Christians as adults. They have
come of age in Christ, and must work out each one his own
discipline in the light of his own special needs and capacities.

In some of his other writings, we find concrete applications of
Paul's flexible approach to the question of discipline. For
instance, though he seems to have believed that in the time
before the end, in which he was living, Christ was calling his
disciples to the celibate state, and although he chose that state
himself, he was too well aware of individual differences to
suppose that this could be a rule for all. For some, the married
state is right. He can say: 'I wish that all were as I myself am.'
Immediately he adds: 'But each one has his special gift from
God, one of one kind and one of another.'[15]

In Christian worship, mission and theology, there will always
be wide diversity. This diversity is itself a testimony to the
creativeness of Christianity. To recognize it and to welcome it is
not indifferentism, for within the diversity there is a unity. But
this unity may be hard to define – it is, shall we say, comparable
to a family likeness.

So while St Paul – and other masters of the spiritual life – have
recognized the peculiarly differing needs of individuals and have
treated disciples as adult and responsible persons, they have
avoided the extremes of individualism. They have recognized
the truth that a spiritual discipline must be freely accepted and
embraced if it is to be fully effective, that worship must be a free
response of love rather than a homage exacted, and yet they
have also looked for some norms by which the various types of
discipline and the forms of worship and devotion can be judged.
For all these ways are meant to converge on a common end –
'mature humanity' in Christ.

Furthermore, although every individual person has his own
unique being, not one of us lives in isolation. Certainly we are
not asked or expected to live the Christian life in isolation, as if
we had to set up for ourselves some rule and then fulfil it as best
we can. That would be discouraging indeed. Our lives are set in
the context of the Christian community, in the body of Christ.
While Paul says that 'each man will have to bear his own load',
in the same passage he also bids us 'bear one another's burdens'.

In the life of the Church, there is mutual support and sharing. There is a growing together toward the 'fulness of Christ', and this is a growing in which the defects of the one are supplemented by the strengths of another. Thus there is a common worship, above all, the offering of the Eucharist, which is the centre and norm to which all private devotions are subordinate.

Individuality and community are poles that run through all aspects of human existence, and they are important in these questions of worship and discipline. Because of the uniqueness of the individual and his special needs, there must be options and the availability of ways suited to this or that particular person. Yet since no man lives to himself, and since no one can be a person except through his relations to other persons, the life of the individual must be embraced (not stifled!) by the life of the community. In the spiritual life, this means that we must be willing to criticize and correct our individual preferences by confronting them with those forms of worship and devotion that have in fact been found fruitful by the community through the centuries in the work of bringing forth the harvest of the Spirit. Although private devotions have a perfectly legitimate place in the texture of Christian spirituality, they are no substitute for common worship. Even in times of persecution, Christians have felt the need to come together for worship, although the risk was great.

So far we have been talking of worship in the life of man, as a discipline or learning process that leads to the sanctification of individual and corporate existence. But we cannot remain satisfied with any account of worship that regards it simply as a training or a psychological exercise. It is true that the practitioners of autosuggestion have compared their therapeutic use of formulas and rituals to the practice of religion, and have claimed for autosuggestion the same effects in the strengthening of will and character. But prayer and worship are more than that. The Christian believes that they are the very ways in which God, the creative mystery from whom we and all things derive their being, comes to us and makes himself present with us. If worship were only a psychological exercise, it would surely be a cumbrous and misleading way of achieving what modern techniques could achieve more readily and intelligibly. But worship is a communing, the opening of human life to God, the response to grace, the growing up into union with God, who has made us for himself.

Some people tell us this is all out of date and neither intelligible nor interesting to contemporary man. They tell us that it is enough for us to have communion with each other, and that in any case the man of our time is incapable of having any sense of a divine presence or of a transcendent Being. It seems to me that such sweeping generalizations cannot be accepted, especially as there seem to be quite a lot of other people around who are searching for an experience of worship.

Let us agree that in the modern world where we have learned to do so much for ourselves and where we live so much of the time in a man-made environment, it may be hard to know what is meant by a 'sense of absolute dependence'. But does not this mean that we should be seeking a more mature and adult understanding of worship and spirituality, rather than throwing them out? Let us agree too that the pressure of modern life has encouraged a pragmatic and even positivist temperament which ties our attention to the tasks at hand and affords little opportunity for meditation on the deeper questions about what we are doing. Are we therefore to capitulate to this state of affairs? Are we to be content with a secularist interpretation of life, and say that communion with God is a thing of the past?

Surely not. Could there even be communion with other people at any depth without both sides being encompassed in a still deeper communion with God? Have the realities of sin and grace and judgment (whatever we may call them) ceased to operate in human life? Can man find a satisfying life without looking beyond the range of the finite and this-worldly?

Tillich once wrote: 'He who is not able to perceive something ultimate, something infinitely significant, is not a man.'[16] This may seem to be just as dogmatic and sweeping an assertion as that of the secularist who dismisses God and the worship of God as relics of a past era of human experience. Are we then simply faced with two assertions? I think we must notice that there is a difference. Tillich has a richer and fuller concept of humanity than those whom he castigates, for he wishes to include a dimension of experience which stretches man to a new stature, while the secularists deny that there is such a dimension and impose narrower limits on what it means to be human. But man, as the self-transcending being, refuses to be arrested at the stage of a truncated nature. If he is deprived of the religious dimension, then he is living as something less than man in the fullest sense. And if our technocratic Western society is inflicting this kind of mutilation upon us, then we must ask what is going wrong with us.

But if it is just a *fact* that many people today are so conditioned that they *cannot* worship or know the joy of being open to transcendence, then is there any point in urging the practice of religion upon them?

I do not think that a fact of this kind is to be accepted as something unalterable. Surely man would have made little progress in the long centuries and millennia of his existence if he had not kept attempting to go beyond the limits that circumscribed his nature at any given time. But the cultural fact of the decline of religion in the modern world is undeniable. If the lack of a religious dimension is, as I have claimed, an impoverishment and a diminution of our humanity, how can one go about the task of opening up this dimension to more people – especially to those who are looking for it, but have not found it?

Obviously the first responsibility lies with those who do practise religion. In the past few decades, the liturgical movement has in fact gone far toward making worship more meaningful to modern persons. Traditional forms have been streamlined and reinterpreted and new experimental forms have been introduced. At the same time theologians have been rethinking the concept of God and his relation to man. If today there are fewer people worshipping than formerly, at least there is some reason to hope that their worship is intelligent and related to the contemporary world.

But in spite of the renewal and reinterpretation of worship that has gone on among Christians, it seems to have had little appeal outside of the Church, even among those who are seeking some form of spirituality. Yet some measure of responsibility lies with them too. No one can say that the capacity for worship and for knowing the presence of God has entirely dried up unless he makes a serious effort to exercise the capacity. It may be that the traditional forms of worship are not helpful to him (in all probability because their meaning has been badly explained to him) but, in that case, let him explore and experiment in the hope of finding a discipline suited to his needs. One obvious way in which such a search may be conducted is to try to enter into the thought and experience of some outstanding contemporary men who have been full participants in the world of today and yet have worked out for themselves and maintained a style of spirituality that gave to their lives and careers a depth and wholeness that they could not otherwise have had. Perhaps there are more people like this than we commonly suppose. Three very different examples of the kind of men I have in mind – three whose contributions to spirituality are briefly discussed in other parts of this book[17] – are Pierre Teilhard de Chardin, priest and scientist; Dag Hammarskjold, statesman and contemplative; Dietrich Bonhoeffer, theologian and political activist. These men are not to be slavishly imitated, but their example may stimulate others to work out their own disciplines, to explore the spiritual dimension of life and to develop the capacity, perhaps long neglected, for knowing God and communing with him.

And only through the exercise of worship can its value be known. It is not simply an indispensable strand in the Christian religion, bringing together faith and action; it is also an enrichment of all human life, lending depth and dignity to man and thereby glorifying God.

Prayer as Thinking

Prayer is at the heart of all religion, but for many Christians prayer has become something of an embarrassment. Is there a place for prayer in the kind of world in which we live? Is prayer a childish exercise which the adult must put from him? Is God, as envisaged in contemporary theology, a God to whom one can still pray, or has prayer gone out with the old anthropomorphic and monarchical images of God?

We are driven to the fundamental question: What is prayer? The question has often been asked, and many answers have been given. Let me then state an answer which can serve as a starting-point for our exploration: *Prayer is thinking*. No single answer tells us the full meaning of prayer or covers all the many kinds of prayer, but every answer contributes something to our understanding of it. Perhaps the answer that prayer is thinking has a special relevance today and will help to resolve some of our perplexities about prayer. While many people have become doubtful about the value of prayer, no one in the age of science and technology and planning questions the value of thinking. Everywhere, there is stress on the need for research, and research implies diligent and sustained thinking. We hear of 'think tanks' being set up, research institutes where men apply their minds to the problems of our society. We even build highly complex 'thinking machines', computers which can think much faster and more efficiently than the human brain. Thinking is as much in fashion as prayer seems out of fashion.

But what if prayer is itself, as I have suggested, a kind of thinking? Obviously it must be a different kind from the utilitarian thinking by which we solve a problem in science or economics, but even if prayer has no evident utilitarian value, it has an indispensable value of its own. It is not a substitute for the hard thinking and hard work by which we must solve our problems, and prayer becomes discredited when it is offered as such a substitute or as a kind of magic short cut to some desired end. But prayer does involve us in a different kind of thinking, a thinking that is essential to human fulfilment. Without this prayerful thinking, all our other thinking, however efficient, falls short of a fully human thinking, and is sometimes in danger of degenerating into mere calculation.

How are we to describe the kind of thinking that is called prayer? Perhaps the first thing to say is that prayer is *passionate* thinking. If there is a thinking that is content to analyse and measure and compare the phenomena of the world, there is also a thinking that enters feelingly into the world and knows itself deeply involved in all that goes on there. Such a thinking is not content to learn what is, but considers what ought to be. It searches for values among the facts, for ideals among the phenomena. Such a thinking is sometimes intermingled with painful longing and desire as it catches the vision of what might be and longs for its realization; sometimes it is suffused with joy and thankfulness as it recognizes great achievement or great horizons of hope and possibility; sometimes it is tinged with shame as we acknowledge that so much of the world's grief and pain has come about 'through my fault, through my own fault, through my own most grievous fault'. This passionate thinking, that is open to feeling the world as well as knowing it, is at least the threshold of prayer. To think of the world with longing for its perfecting is a step toward praying for the coming of the king-dom; to think of the world with rejoicing for all that is good is inarticulately to hallow the name; to think of the world with shame for our failures is implicitly to ask forgiveness of our sins and trespasses. Wherever there is the kind of passionate thinking described above, there is something that has an affinity with prayer. One gladly acknowledges this affinity, while recognizing that some of those who engage in such passionate thinking are unwilling to call it prayer, and that such thinking must be accorded an integrity of its own. When a serious-minded humanist thinks passionately of the world in the light of his ideals, he is not indeed praying but he is engaging in a spiritual exercise not far removed from prayer.

Prayer is not only passionate thinking, it is *compassionate* thinking. In prayer, we go out from ourselves, we stand alongside the other, we try to share his feelings and aspirations. In Buddhist spirituality, there is a meditative practice known as the *Brahma-vihara*, an expression which could quite properly be translated as 'dwelling with reality'. Prayer is not, as is sometimes alleged, a flight or an escape from reality. It is a dwelling with reality in the sense of a compassionate confrontation in thought with human beings in their actual situations. The Buddhist monk thinks in turn of the four corners of the earth with their teeming inhabitants. He directs his mind toward them first with friendship, next with compassion, then with sympathy and finally with equanimity.

In recent years we have heard quite often of 'sensitivity training' and within the Church there have been courses in such training for clergy and others, designed to make people more aware of each other and more open to each others' needs. Some of the methods employed in such training have been questionable, but I should think that one very important way of heightening sensitivity would be the discipline of compassionate thinking.

For the Christian, compassionate thinking takes the form of intercessory prayer, a compassionate confrontation with the needs of the other in the presence of God. Intercessory prayer includes compassionate thinking, but it is something more and implies the belief that in such prayer not only the person who prays is sensitized and stimulated to action but that the power of God himself is somehow related to the situation which is the concern of the prayer. Such a belief clearly raises both theological and practical difficulties – theological difficulties in conceiving the relation of God to the world and its history, and practical difficulties arising from the temptation to turn such prayer into an egotistical and magical manipulation of God. But the difficulties are not insuperable and the Christian who takes the New Testament seriously is surely committed to belief in intercessory prayer and to the practice of it. Basically, it seems to me that intercessory prayer provides, as it were, openings into the dense texture of the human situation through which can come the

creative and healing power of the reality we call God; and because within that human situation our lives are all bound together
in a mysterious solidarity, then God's power is able to operate far
beyond the particular person who offers the prayer, though
through him. Prayer, as petition and intercession, helps to make
the human reality porous to the divine reality – the whole
human reality, and not only that part of it actively engaged in
prayer.

Of course, it needs hardly to be said that intercessory prayer
and likewise the compassionate thinking of Buddhists, humanists and others, makes no sense unless it is matched by action
directed toward the realization of wholeness, health, peace,
salvation. But if such prayer is a dwelling with reality and an
openness to its claims upon us, it can hardly fail to stimulate
action. Compassionate thinking is dangerous for anyone who
wants to stay wrapped up in himself. It draws people out of
themselves, and the results have sometimes been dramatic.
Father Damien and Albert Schweitzer are famous examples of
men led by compassionate thinking to give up security in order
to dwell with the reality of the poor, the sick, the repulsive. But
even when the results are not dramatic, the compassionate confrontation with the other in prayer must lead to the increase of
sympathy and the upbuilding of community.

Prayer is also *responsible* thinking. In using the language of
responsibility, I am drawing attention again to something we
noticed in connection with compassion, namely, that prayer is
a thinking that takes us out of ourselves. Responsibility is
answerability. In prayer we are answering or responding to
what lies beyond ourselves and makes a claim upon us.

Responsibility to the neighbour is the best-known kind of
responsibility. No one can live to himself; he must take account
of the needs and claims of the neighbour. The *considerate* person,
as we call him, is the person who considers or thinks responsibly
of the neighbour. Just as in the case of compassionate thinking,
so in the present case we must recognize that there is responsible
thinking which is not prayer, though it is akin to prayer and
even a kind of threshold to prayer. But in prayer one acknowledges a responsibility that goes beyond even the neighbour and
draws one even further out of oneself. This is responsibility
before God. I have talked of prayer as a 'dwelling with reality'.

But 'God' is the name by which religious faith designates the ultimate reality, the final mystery of being. Prayer is our responsible thinking in the presence of God. In prayer we know God as the unconditioned demand made upon us – though, to be sure, this demand is mediated through some finite situation. Our response is the prayer of faith and commitment, or the supplication for grace.

Sometimes we know God as the undeserved grace that sustains us, and then our response takes a somewhat different form. It is the response of thanksgiving, and in such cases prayer is a *thankful* thinking – the lifting up of our hearts in thanksgiving for whatever is good in the creation and for whatever promises of something still better are held out to us.

In talking about prayer that goes out from the self to acknowledge responsibility before God or to give thanks to God, have we come to forms that are meaningful only to the believer? We have already seen that humanists and non-Christians sometimes engage in spiritual exercises that are not far removed from prayer, and perhaps this witnesses to an inclination to pray in the heart of every man. But when the Christian consciously directs his prayers of faith and thanksgiving to God, has he entered a territory quite unknown to those who do not share his faith?

Certainly, there is a sense in which Christian prayer is distinctive, and the acknowledgement and exploration of this distinctiveness is just as important as drawing attention to the affinities between Christian prayer and non-Christian spirituality. The Christian believes that the mystery of God is opened up in Jesus Christ, so that it is in Christ that we experience both the ultimate demand and the ultimate grace, and it is through Christ that prayer is offered. Later we shall consider at greater length prayer centred on Jesus Christ.[1]

But for the moment, I want to point out that even those prayers in which we acknowledge responsibility before God or offer thanks to God have remarkable parallels among persons who may not be willing to speak of God at all. Close to the responsible thinking of which I have been speaking is a practice described by Iris Murdoch, who writes: 'I think there is a place both inside and outside religion for a sort of contemplation of the Good, not just by dedicated experts but by ordinary people;

an attention which is not just the planning of particular good actions but an attempt to look right away from self towards a distant transcendent perfection, a source of uncontaminated energy, a source of *new* and quite undreamt of virtue.'[2] As an illustration of thankful thinking, let me cite a case from my own experience. Some years ago, a certain professor of philosophy was killed in an automobile accident. As one of his closest friends, I was asked to conduct the memorial service. As I knew that he was not a Christian in the conventional sense and that many of those present at the funeral would be agnostics, I thought that it would be unreal and possibly an offence to his integrity just to read the Burial Office. Yet I also considered that it would be woefully inadequate and false to my own beliefs were I merely to deliver a eulogy. So, among other things, I invited all present to join in an act of thanksgiving for our departed brother, an act in which we recalled with thanks his many gifts and his many thankworthy deeds. This thankful thinking, I believe, was truly an act of prayer. It was so explicitly for those of us who were giving thanks to God. But was it not also prayer for those who simply gave thanks . . . without specifying to whom or to what? At least, the act joined us together in a spiritual exercise without infringing the integrity of any.

One could say many more things about prayer and about the kinds of thinking in which it involves us. It is a mere caricature of prayer to regard it as emergency signals which we send out to God in difficult situations. Prayer is a fundamental style of thinking, passionate and compassionate, responsible and thankful, that is deeply rooted in our humanity and that manifests itself not only among believers but also among serious-minded people who do not profess any religious faith. Yet it seems to me that if we follow out the instinct to pray that is in all of us, it will finally bring us to faith in God. Michael Novak remarks: 'It is in prayer that one comes to know God best.'[3] And he goes on to ask the very significant question, whether people do not pray because they do not believe in God, or whether they do not believe in God because they have given up (or never learned) prayer. To pray is to think in such a way that we dwell with reality, and faith's name for reality is God.

2

In the first section of this chapter, I have described prayer as a form of thinking, and have tried to show that even persons who do not profess any religious faith sometimes engage in ways of thinking that are very near to prayer. I think this fact alone indicates that even in our contemporary secularized world, people experience a deep need for prayer, though this need may not always be recognized for what it is.

But among some people the prejudice against prayer is nowadays so great that we must consider in greater detail what is the place of prayer and what are the claims of prayer today. We live in the age of autonomous man. More and more he has taken over control of his life and his environment. God the creator surely meant him to do this, and we are right to accept ever-increasing responsibilities for the world and to extend our rule over the forces of nature. But we are wrong if, in the midst of all this, we come to believe that prayer is a weakness that should be put behind us or a childish habit that should be outgrown. Mature prayer is by no means opposed to human responsibility, or to an adult and sophisticated attitude toward the world. On the contrary, mature prayer (but it must be mature!) strengthens and deepens responsibility and gives a clearer vision of the tasks that have to be done.

How is it possible to make such claims for prayer? I believe they can be vindicated if we take a closer look at the times in which we are living, with all their promise and all their danger. I believe we shall find that prayer is one of our most solid grounds for hoping that the promise will be fulfilled and the danger overcome.

It is often said that we live in a time of fragmentation. This is true in innumerable ways. In the complex society of a modern industrial state, each person has to become competent in some highly specialized task. He has to be preoccupied with developing and improving his own particular skills, and he has little time or energy to extend his knowledge and experience to other areas. A man is what he does, and what he does is so limited and circumscribed that no clear goal or purpose seems to be in view. This is the 'functional man', and although some philosophers have criticized this type of humanity, notably Gabriel Marcel, it seems inevitable that to some extent we must all be functional men and women nowadays. We play a limited number of roles, and in each of these we deal with a succession of tasks interspersed with enjoyments and sometimes with sufferings. These tasks come along one after the other, with little apparent connection with one another, and, as the pace of life keeps increasing, we find ourselves living in a whirl of events that do not seem to add up to anything that makes sense.

But there is a strange contradiction in the human condition today. Alongside the increasing specialization and fragmentation of the functional man we find at work factors that keep drawing us into ever-increasing closeness and interdependence. So simple an operation as shopping in a supermarket is made possible by a worldwide network of enormous complexity, involving industries, transportation systems, communications, political arrangements, banking and financial organizations, together with the untold numbers of people who in one way or another contribute to the smooth working of the system. We have become so used to this great network that for most of the time we remain quite unconscious of it. Only when it is threatened with a breakdown, as, for instance, when a city is paralysed by a power failure or a heavy snowstorm, do we suddenly realize to what an extent we have all become members of one body.

Because of our fragmentation and individualism, we are ill prepared to meet the new demand that we should be able to see things as a whole and that we should be able to experience more wholeness in our own lives. We find ourselves in one world, but our mental training has been such that our attention is riveted on one little area. Yet the kind of world in which we live demands that we 'think big', so to speak, and recover a sense of the cosmic dimensions of existence. The ecological crisis is an obvious symptom of the imbalance that has arisen between the preoccupation with limited problems on the one hand and the need to conceive ever larger unities on the other. Marshall McLuhan writes: 'Indifference to the cosmic fosters intense concentration on minute segments and specialist tasks, which is the unique strength of Western man. For the specialist is the one who never makes small mistakes while moving toward the grand fallacy.'[4] This sums up admirably the predicament we are in.

The 'unique strength' of the functional man which enabled him to concentrate successfully on his limited tasks is turning into a unique threat that may deprive him of that wholeness of vision which he needs for the new age. Somehow the wall separating the compartments into which we have divided life must be broken down or, at least, made porous so that each part can be seen to make sense within a larger whole.

The religious believer may fairly claim that prayer is one important way in which wholeness may be recovered. To pray is not only to think, it is to 'think big'. Prayerful thinking is a thinking which crosses barriers and establishes connections between things that were separate and persons who were estranged or indifferent. The wholeness fostered by prayerful thinking is twofold.

On the one hand, it brings wholeness to the life of the person who prays. When we take time to pray, the succession of activities in which we all too often engage unthinkingly is brought into the focus of thought. We take time to establish priorities, to set goals, to eliminate contradictions, to ask about where we are going. To think of these things in the presence of God and in the light of Christ is already to experience a meaning in life and to let our many separate acts be brought together in a connected unity. Prayer is itself an activity of the whole man, and in turn it promotes his growth in wholeness. To lay one's life before God in prayer is already to have faith that in spite of its failures and inconsistencies, in spite even of its seeming absurdities and trivialities, it can become a meaningful contribution to God's universe.

On the other hand, prayer helps us to see the world as a whole. Although perhaps we do not often think of it in this way, prayer is not very far removed from theology. Both are reflective, meditative acts. They are forms of thinking in which we ponder the meaning of faith. To have faith is to meet the world with the conviction that in spite of all its ambiguities and its downright evils, there can be discerned in it the reality of love and a ground of hope. Prayer helps to integrate our vision of the world, just as it helps to integrate our own lives. Some people were surprised when it was learned that Dag Hammarskjold, who was killed in Africa while seeking peace as Secretary-General of the United Nations, had been a man of prayer and of a deep spirituality, as was revealed in his diaries. But why should anyone have been surprised – at any rate, anyone with the faintest inkling of what prayer means? Without prayer and meditation, how could one ever hope to see a possibility of unity amid all the conflicting facts of the contemporary world, or how could one ever have a vision of peace, for peace simply means wholeness and fulfilment?

So I am claiming that prayer enables us to see things in perspective, to attain the vision of them in their unity and interrelatedness rather than as just so many separate items. Prayer changes our vision of the world, and so influences our action in it. Some contemporary writers on spirituality might challenge me at this point, for it has become fashionable to say that the direction of spirituality is not from inside to outside, but from outside to inside; or, to put the matter in another way, that we do not go from prayer to the world but confront the world directly and then learn to pray. It seems to me that those who talk in this way have set up a mistaken disjunction. They assume that prayer and the world, thought and action, are separate and have to be brought together, so then they have to ask which comes first. The very question indicates that wholeness has been missed. The truth is that prayer and action, the inward and the outward, are bound together in such a close reciprocity that it makes no sense to ask which comes first. They are in constant interaction. Prayer interprets the world, and the world interprets prayer.

This has always been understood by masters of the spiritual life. The mystic John Eckhart remarked: 'No person in this life may reach the point at which he can be excused from outward service. Even if he is given to a life of contemplation, still he cannot refrain from going out and taking an active part in life.'[5] Alongside these words from the fourteenth century, one may set these from the twentieth, taken from Hammarskjold's diary: 'The longest journey is the journey inward' and 'the road to holiness necessarily passes through the world of action.'[6]

Prayer does not take place in a vacuum, but in the real world; but that very world would itself be vacuous if it were not seen in the light of prayer. This remark applies just as much to the world of today as to the worlds of earlier times. The more complex our world becomes and the more extensively man's power over the world grows, the more we need the vision of wholeness which prayer brings.

3

There are many forms of prayer and many levels of prayer. Some people find one form more helpful than another, and we should never criticize another person simply because his needs and his ways of satisfying them are different from our own. Again, because prayer has many levels, there are some kinds of prayer that we cannot appreciate, still less criticize, until we have ourselves passed through the stages that lead to such prayer and have learned for ourselves what it really is.

In the earlier sections of this chapter I have cast the net broadly, and written about prayer in a general way. Now I wish to turn to a particular kind of prayer and to a particular Christian form of it. I mean contemplative prayer, and especially contemplative prayer in the sacramental presence of Christ. Such prayer has to be learned, and those who have learned it and understood it set immense value upon it. It has for long had an honourable place in catholic spirituality. But seen only from the outside, it is easily misunderstood. It has been assailed in the past as superstitious but in the activist temper of our own time it is more likely to be criticized as quietist. Since our concern is to find a spirituality that can stand up to the modern critique of religion, we must face these criticisms honestly. I think they can all be fairly answered, and in the course of answering them we shall find ourselves deepening our understanding of this form of prayer, and for some it may even be that their attachment to it will be strengthened.

There are three main criticisms that I hear from time to time from some of my own friends. First, they may ask: 'What really is this "contemplation" of which religious people speak? Is it not just a kind of fuzzy lack of precision, letting the mind go blank, sinking into some sort of daze or tranquillizing day-dream?' A second critical question is this: 'Should we not see Christ's presence everywhere, in the street and in the neighbour, rather than in the Host upon the altar? Are we not imprisoning him in the church?' And finally they may ask: 'Is not contemplative prayer before the Sacrament really a selfish indulgence for people who happen to like it, like listening to music or even luxuriating in a warm bath, when they ought to be out in the world doing the will of God?' These questions do have their point, and it is good that they are asked, as they serve to warn us that sacramental devotion (like everything else) can become distorted. But they miss the main point and betray an imperfect understanding, as I shall try to show in responding to each of them in turn.

First, then, is 'contemplation' just an impressive word for a blank state of mind? To answer this, let us first consider an analogy. We have all seen two young people fall in love. To begin with, they are silent in each other's presence. A shyness inhibits speech. They want to say things to each other, but the mind goes blank and they cannot yet declare themselves. Then one day a level of confidence is reached where the floodgates of speech are opened. Now they cannot find enough time for all they have to say. They hear each other's history and plans over and over again, they spend endless hours in exchanging confidences and exploring each other's mind. But eventually silence returns. However, this is a new kind of silence. It is not the silence of the blank mind, the mind that has yet to speak. It is the silence of the full mind, when all has been spoken and summed up and understood, and a new level of communing has been established.

So it is with prayer. There is the inarticulate silence of the prayer that has not yet been uttered. The desire to pray is stirring in the mind, but the mind is still blank, the prayer has no content, words do not come, we are still at the stage of the disciples when they said, 'Lord, teach us to pray.'[7] Then comes the stage of verbal prayer. We learn the words: 'Our Father!' A vast area of prayer now opens before us and through words and language we immerse ourselves in God and our relation to him is built up and strengthened. Perhaps especially important here are those forms of prayer called meditative prayer, where we rehearse the mighty acts of God in the mysteries of Christ and meditate upon them.[8] We get to know God in Christ, and this kind of exploration can never come to an end, for we are exploring that which is inexhaustible. Yet sometimes we find that verbal prayer does run out into silence. But this is a silence quite different from the inarticulate silence which held us before we learned the language of prayer. Now we have come to what

Karl Jaspers has finely called 'the silence of fulfilled speech'.[9] All that has been said and all that has been absorbed in the successive moments of meditation is now present together in an ineffable fulness to which words are inadequate. This is contemplation – a moment we may not know very often, but one in which the mind, so far from being blank, overflows with the fulness of divine truth. We are given a foretaste here and now of the vision of God, the vision that gathers up everything in itself.

The Eucharist in a unique and wonderful way leads us through the many truths about God and his dealings with us in Christ. Our minds grasp these truths one at a time, and the liturgy presents them to us and involves us in them in the most effective order. Ideally, they should all burst upon us at once, in a McLuhanesque simultaneity, and some current experiments in liturgy aim at achieving this. But this is also how we may understand the meaning of contemplative prayer before the reserved Sacrament. The Host gathers up and concentrates the whole eucharistic action and the whole eucharistic truth, and our silent adoration before the Host is the way in which we let our minds be seized and filled with a presence – a presence whom we indeed know and with whom we have conversed and on whose deeds we have meditated, but a presence who in his immediate fulness makes all further words superfluous.

The second critical question can be answered more briefly. It was the question whether we should not seek the presence of Christ in the streets and in the neighbour rather than in the Sacrament. Certainly, we must acknowledge that Christ can be encountered anywhere. But I do think that we need a focus where we encounter him face to face if we are to learn to recognize him in other places where he may be hard to discern. Most of us have far too little sensitivity to Christ in the world, and unless we get some training in sensitivity, he may elude us altogether. I could walk around Piccadilly Circus or Times Square for hours, among the garish scenes and the fevered crowds, and, left to myself, I doubt if I would ever have any sense of God or Christ in such places. But if I watch for a little hour in Christ's sacramental presence, exposed to the essence and concentrated fulness of his saving life and death and resurrection, then I hope I shall begin to acquire the kind of sensitivity that will enable me to recognize and respond to Christ in situations where his presence is not obvious. Bernard Häring truly writes, 'Only prayer can sensitize a man to the apostolic possibilities of the present situation.'[10]

The foregoing remarks have already begun to answer the final critical question, which was whether contemplation is a luxury which we choose to enjoy rather than going out and doing God's will. Let it be frankly acknowledged that the desire to linger in Christ's presence is a strong one – and why not? We remember the story of Martha and Mary, and also the desire of the disciples to linger on the Mount of Transfiguration. Always it will be needful in the Church for some to devote themselves to contemplation, and they do it for all. But most of us find our vocations in the world, and it is there that we have the duty of doing the will of the Father and going out at the command of Christ to participate in his mission. But I think that if we understand properly the nature of contemplative prayer (whether before the Sacrament or in some other form), we shall understand also that it is our great source of strength for going out in obedience to Christ. Indeed, I am bound to say from my own observation that those Christian activists who make much of mission but little or nothing of prayer are rarely themselves good representatives of the Christian mission. They tend to become hard, self-righteous and a little fanatical, and lack the serenity and inward strength which ought to characterize the Christian approach. Mark Gibbard has a perceptive comment to make: 'When I see many people so incessantly involved . . . I feel concerned about them. I am anxious for them – and not only for them, but for those whom they are trying to help. I cannot help wondering whether in this ceaseless demand on their physical and nervous resources they can keep a true sense of proportion. Is it possible that they might be more truly and effectively involved if they had, under normal circumstances, times of disinvolvement?'[11] Of course, these 'times of disinvolvement', if we think of them as times of prayer, could also be described as times of involvement in a different way – an involvement of thinking which is not opposed to but complementary to an involvement of action. Those times of prayer set up a frame of mind which remains through all our activities, so that, as Herbert Waddams has expressed it, 'all our work and play is coloured by a prayerlike attitude'.[12]

The relation of contemplative prayer to faithful witness in the world can be studied in some of the figures who have been caught up in the tragic events of our own century. Many people in this country have heard of Dietrich Bonhoeffer and his death at the hands of the Nazis, but not so many have heard of his fellow resister, Albrecht Haushofer, a lay professor just about Bonhoeffer's own age and killed by the Nazis in the same month.[13] In the months before his death, Haushofer was imprisoned in the infamous Moabit jail in Berlin, and there he wrote a number of poems. In one of them he tells how one night in his cell he had a vision of the calm face of the great Buddha of Kamakura. This is what he read in that face:

> He knew no anger, no despair.
> He taught just one thing – how we should sink,
> How we should direct our individual wills
> Into the great will.[14]

What Haushofer saw in the Buddha was what he needed for himself – not sheer resignation, but the courage and calm to carry through his witness to the end, to submit his will to the great will, and all without anger or despair. But Haushofer did not need to turn to Eastern religion or sink himself in Buddhist meditation in his quest, for Christianity too has its tradition of contemplation, even if this has been undervalued and neglected. The kind of prayer of which I have been writing in this section is precisely the kind in which we sink ourselves in Christ, the one who himself prayed, 'Not my will, but thine!'[15] To be doing the will of God rather than one's own is the hardest thing in the world. No one can do it without the aid of the divine grace. Contemplative prayer in the sacramental presence of Christ is one fruitful way in which we can be conformed to him and sent out to do his bidding.

> Praised, blessed and adored be Jesus Christ!
> On his throne in heaven,
> In the most holy Sacrament of the altar,
> And in the hearts of his people.

'Only prayer can wear away our native resistance to God.'[16]

Spirit and Spirituality

In this chapter we take up the meaning of spirituality. The word 'spirituality' is used in a broad way, and includes prayer, worship and whatever other practices are associated with the development of the spiritual life. But just as prayer and worship have become suspect, so too 'spirituality' has become a word of doubtful repute. To some it suggests a kind of hot-house atmosphere in which people are unduly preoccupied with their own inward condition. To others it suggests a pale ghostly semi-existence in which the spiritual is contrasted with the bodily and material. To others again, the word has connotations of unctuousness and pseudo-piety. Yet, in spite of all misunderstandings, the word 'spirituality' still has a certain fascination and it has been rediscovered by some of the young people. This is because it points to something so important that no amount of distortion and perversion can ever quite destroy it. I believe that fundamentally spirituality has to do with *becoming a person in the fullest sense*, and the rest of the chapter will be devoted to exploring what this means.

We begin by pushing the problem further back. To talk about 'spirituality' would seem to imply that we already understand what is meant by the word 'spirit'. Yet the word 'spirit' is notoriously difficult and ambiguous. It is a word which (except in the expression 'Holy Spirit') I have usually avoided in my own theological writings, precisely because of the difficulty of attaching a clear meaning to it.

But I can scarcely avoid it in a writing devoted to spirituality! Let us begin then by noting that the term 'spirit', like many other items in the religious vocabulary, was originally an image or picture rather than a concept. The image was, of course, that of the stirring of the air: the breath or the breeze.[1] The breath is the invisible though none the less palpable characteristic that distinguishes a living man from a dead one; the breeze is the equally invisible force that stirs around man in the world and that manifests itself in many effects there. Walther Eichrodt remarks: 'No wonder, then, that in the blowing of the wind and in the rhythm of human respiration the ancients detected a divine mystery, and saw in this element in Nature, at once so near to him and yet so incomprehensible, a symbol of the mysterious nearness and activity of the divine.'[2]

The general significance of the imagery is clear enough. It was already bringing to expression the conviction that to reality there belongs a depth, a complexity and a richness that are not exhausted by the visible and material objects presented to the senses. Man is more than his physical body, and man's environment is more than the physical universe. But if 'spirit' is understood as more than the physical, it is not separated from the material world in some 'beyond', but shows itself in the world and even enters into the body of man.

Furthermore, the biblical imagery of spirit is essentially dynamic. The breath and the breeze are in motion. Spirit is the active, formative, lifegiving power. Language about the 'indwelling' spirit is inadequate if its suggests a merely passive inhabiting. The Old Testament idea of spirit, in Oliver Quick's words, 'represents an invasive, rather than a pervasive, power'.[3]

It is a far cry from the early Hebrew imagery of the breath and the breeze to the subtle concepts of spirit which have been developed in Western philosophy, both ancient and modern. Some of these philosophical concepts of spirit stand in rather sharp opposition to the Old Testament ideas, especially when they have set up a dichotomy between spirit and matter and have conceived these as different kinds of substance. At the same time, it must be remembered that possibly the greatest of all European philosophies of spirit, that of Hegel, agreed with the Old Testament in refusing to isolate the spiritual from the physical and in seeing the former as the dynamic reality which expresses itself in the latter: 'Nature is far from being so fixed and complete as to subsist without spirit. And similarly spirit on its part is not merely a world beyond nature and nothing more;

it is really and with full proof seen to be spirit only when it involves nature as absorbed in itself.'[4]

No concept of spirit can be adequate to the reality. Spirit is 'incomprehensible', in the sense in which that adjective is used in the English version of the Athanasian creed. It does not mean that we can have no understanding of the matter at all, but it does mean that the full significance of spirit always breaks out beyond the grasp of our concepts. This is clearer when we remember that 'incomprehensible' is a not very felicitous translation of the Latin *immensus*, meaning that which cannot be measured or contained in the categories of finite thought. Spirit has an elusive character. 'The wind blows where it will, and you hear the sound of it, but cannot tell whence it comes or whither it goes.'[5]

The imagery of the biblical language, evocative rather than precisely descriptive, well suggests the elusiveness of spirit itself. But we do need to clarify our language as much as possible, especially if we have any intention of commending spirituality to those who have become uncertain or even suspicious about it. And it should not be impossible to reach some clarification. From the beginning, the Spirit of God has been understood as God amidst humanity, God present and active in the world, God in his closeness to us as a dynamic reality shaping human lives and histories. The Spirit, in this sense, is not something other than God, but God in that manner of the divine Being in which he comes closest, dwells with us, acts upon us. When one considers the matter from this point of view, it would seem much more difficult to form any interpretative concept of the Father than it would of the Spirit, among the Persons of the Trinity. For although the image of the Father seems more concrete and definite than the image of the Wind or Breath, yet the mysterious source of all beings, the deepest and ultimate region of the Godhead, is surely more remote and inaccessible than the Spirit who moves among us and whose spiritual being is somehow shared by us. The New Testament declares that it is through the Spirit that we have access to the Father[6] and that it is by the 'Spirit of adoption' that we are empowered to cry 'Abba, Father'.[7]

More than that, as mentioned in the last paragraph, 'spirit' names a kind of being that is somehow shared by man with the Spirit of God. Spirit is present in and constitutive of man, as well as God. The word points to the mysterious affinity that binds man to God, an affinity that has to be affirmed just as strongly as the otherness which differentiates God from man. When God had made man a creature of the dust, he 'breathed into his nostrils the breath of life; and man became a living soul.'[8] Thus man, alone among all the beings on earth, was granted a share of spirit. He has not only learned to perceive the Spirit of God without; he recognizes that there is spirit within. Thus, because of our share in spirit given in creation, we should be able to find within ourselves, in the very structure of our being, some clue to the nature of the divine Spirit. It is true, of course, that man's spiritual endowment is often sadly obscured because he immerses himself in sensual indulgences or in amassing possessions. It is true also that spirit itself can become perverted so that we can speak of 'evil spirit' and of 'spiritual evil', and these represent a pitch of sin beyond sensuality. Yet the true potentialities of spirit are never quite abolished. So long as there is a recognizably human experience, there can be discerned the lineaments of spirit as given by God in creation.

Let us proceed then to consider what it is that makes us spiritual beings. What can we say about spirit as the most elusive and mysterious constituent of our human nature, yet the one that seems most distinctive when we think of man in relation to all the other beings on earth? If we can form a clearer idea of spirit as we are aware of it on the level of our own experience, then we should be able in turn to attain a clearer understanding of the Spirit of God and finally of the meaning of spirituality.

We have already taken note that when we talk of 'spirit' in man, we are pointing to that extra dimension of being that belongs to him and that makes him more than a mere physical organism or a highly complicated animal. We do not relate to other people as if they were only objects that we could see and hear and touch or even as if they were simply living organisms from which reactions could be evoked. We relate to them *as persons*, and we talk about them or talk to them in a language appropriate to persons. What makes the difference between a person and a thing or between a person and an animal is not itself something that can be seen. It is the invisible 'extra dimension' as I have called it, and we know this at first hand in our experiences of thinking, willing, feeling, experiences which we attribute to other human beings as well. It is this range of experience that is distinctive of the human being and that we call 'spirit'.

We need not suppose, as some philosophers have done, that spirit is some kind of substance, to be contrasted with physical substance. Nowadays at least, to talk of anything as a 'substance' almost inevitably suggests that it is some kind of 'thing'. But to reify spirit is surely to commit a category mistake. Furthermore, to reify spirit tends to reduce it to the ontological level of that very thinghood beyond which, as we have suggested, the image of spirit was meant to point to a different dimension of reality. Talk of 'spirit' was meant to express the perception that reality is not exhausted by the things we discern by the senses. However, our minds are so much under the domination of the category of thinghood that we immediately tend to convert spirit itself into another thing. But spirit is not another thing, not another substance parallel to the substance of physical entities. Spirit belongs to a different category. It is, we might say, a dynamic form, just as life, for instance, is not a thing but a special form and a distinct mode of being.

What then is this dynamic form or mode of being which we call 'spirit' and which we know in the human experience? It may be described as a capacity for going out of oneself and beyond oneself; or, again, as the capacity for transcending oneself. Human beings are not closed or shut up in themselves. They are not just objects among the objects that make up the world, with a given nature and destiny. To them there belong essentially freedom and creativity, whereby they are able to shape (within limits) both themselves and their world. It is this openness, freedom, creativity, this capacity for going beyond any given state in which they find themselves, that makes possible self-consciousness and self-criticism, understanding, responsibility, the pursuit of knowledge, the sense of beauty, the quest of the good, the formation of community, the outreach of love and whatever else belongs to the amazing richness of what we call the 'life of the spirit'. And, as already said, though sin severely impairs this life, it never destroys it or humanity would cease to be.

The kind of openness and self-transcendence of which I have been writing is what existentialist philosophers have called 'existence', in the strong sense of that word as an 'ex-sisting' or

'standing out'. It is this 'ex-sisting' that is the peculiar characteristic of man's mode of being, and clearly it is closely related to
'spirit', as described above. But perhaps the dynamic character
of spirit could be even better expressed if, instead of talking of
'existence' as 'standing out', I were to coin a new word and say
that spirit is *exience*, that is to say, 'going out'.[9] The word
'exience' would better express the essentially dynamic form of
spiritual being as continually going out from itself.

The more man goes out from himself or goes beyond himself,
the more the spiritual dimension of his life is deepened, the more
he becomes truly man, the more also he grows in likeness to
God, who is Spirit. On the other hand, the more he turns inward and encloses himself in self-interest, the less human does
he become. This is the strange paradox of spiritual being – that
precisely by going out and spending itself, it realizes itself. It
grows not weaker but stronger, for it is not a quantifiable thing.

It is worth noting that the Greek word cognate with 'existence' is '*ek-stasis*'. The life of the spirit is therefore the 'ecstatic'
life, precisely the life that goes out of itself. But just as I have
claimed that 'exience' would be a more dynamic term than
'existence', so I think we can find a better word than 'ecstasis'.
The adjective 'ecstatic' is especially too strongly reminiscent of
'static', the very opposite of 'dynamic'. I suggest we might do
better to speak of 'ecbasis' and 'ecbatic' to capture the notion
of a genuine surging forth of spirit.[10]

In saying that the life of the spirit is ecbatic (or ecstatic), I do
not mean by this that it is a life marked by sporadic periods of
intense experience. One might get this impression, admittedly,
from passages in the Old Testament which tell of prophets who
were, so to speak, 'beside themselves' in their moments of
prophesying, and the Hebrew word for such a prophet, *nabi*,
means one who raves or speaks ecstatically. Even in the New
Testament we read about such intense moments of Spirit-
possession as issued in 'speaking with tongues'. It is hardly
surprising that today, in a world that has been starved of
spirituality, many people are turning to the intense spirit-
experiences of the Pentecostalist sects. However, the main tendency in the New Testament is to see the work of the Spirit and
thus a truly spiritual life for man as manifested in the less
sensational but ethically more important 'gifts' or 'fruits' of the

Spirit – love, joy, peace, patience, kindness, goodness, faithfulness, gentleness, self-control.[11] These gifts are not confined to
exceptional spirit-filled individuals but are distributed throughout the body of Christ. To those who make up that body,
St Paul can say that 'to each is given the manifestation of the
Spirit for the common good'.[12] Yet while there is nothing
sensational or psychologically abnormal about these *charismata*,
as compared with the more frenzied manifestations of possession
by the Spirit, the gifts are none the less ecstatic (or ecbatic) in
the strict sense. They draw the recipient out of himself into a
new manner of life. He goes out from a self-centred mode of
being into a new openness. The merely 'natural' life is broken
open and the 'spiritual' man is born. This is the spiritual
rebirth. 'That which is born of the Spirit is spirit.'[13] It is not a
rebirth once for all but a continuing process of rebirth and
renewal.

In stressing that the highest fruits or gifts of the Spirit are not
sensational performances but ethical qualities, I am also stressing the personal character of spirit, both in God and man. Some
early ideas of the Spirit of the Lord seem to have supposed that
this was some impersonal force that might take possession of a
man and cause him to do extraordinary things quite apart from
his own volition. But the Christian understanding of the Spirit
thinks of his action as the personal action of God upon men.
Such action does not force men into strange patterns of behaviour, and it does not suspend their exercise of reason and
will. Rather, it heightens whatever in man is spiritual – his
rationality, freedom and creativity. The approach is on the
personal level through reason and conscience, and the response
is no involuntary submission to a strange power but rather a
willing and fully personal going out to join in the life of a Spirit
greater than man's.

The words 'spirit' and 'person' are not synonymous. Obviously,
for instance, a human person is not simply a spirit. He is also a
creature of flesh and blood. Yet person and spirit, though not
identical, are closely connected. Spirit is the most distinctive
constituent of personhood. We might say that spirit is the form
of the personal.

Personal rebirth is the work of the divine Spirit, but it is also
the fulfilling and perfecting of the basically spiritual constitution

of man, the 'existent' being who has a freedom and a creativity that make him more than just another item in the inventory of created things. Man 'stands out' from all other creatures on earth and has the possibility of exience, of going out and transcending himself into a fuller form of life. This possibility was his from the moment that breath or spirit was breathed into him by God, bestowing on him the divine image and the possibility of closeness to God and participation in the divine life. Already then we have gone far toward establishing the thesis announced at the beginning of this chapter, that spirituality is, in simple terms, the process of becoming a person in the fullest sense.

But now that we have spent a little time exploring the meaning of spirit as we know it in human life, let us see whether what we have learned can provide an analogy, however fragmentary, by which we may arrive at a better understanding of the Spirit of God and so finally at a still more adequate understanding of spirituality.

We have learned that when we talk of 'spirit' in man, we refer to his capacity for going out beyond himself. It would seem then that we must also think of the divine Spirit in terms of God's openness, of his exience or going out. And at once we must be struck with the fact that the language we use about the Holy Spirit is precisely the language of 'going out', of 'procession'. He is 'the Spirit of truth, who proceeds (*ekporeuetai*) from the Father'.[14] In the familiar words of the Nicene Creed in its Western form, the Holy Spirit 'proceeds from the Father and the Son'.

Although the important point for my argument is simply the notion of procession, I should perhaps pause for a moment to say something about the vexed question of a single or a double procession. I mention the matter because it has implications for spirituality as well as for systematic theology.

It is well-known that in the original version of the Nicene creed, the Holy Spirit was said to proceed from the Father, without any mention of the Son. In this respect, it agreed with the verse from St John's Gospel, quoted above. But some early theologians (mostly, but not all, in the West) began to teach that the Spirit proceeds from the Father and the Son, the doctrine now known as that of the double procession. St Cyril of Alexandria, for instance, wrote: 'For though the Holy Spirit has a personal subsistence of his own and is conceived of by himself, in that he is the Spirit and not the Son, yet he is not therefore alien from the Son. For he is called "the Spirit of Truth" and Christ is "the Truth", and he is poured forth from him (Christ) just as he also is from God the Father.'[15] This doctrine came to be accepted in the West and was incorporated into the creed by the addition of the *filioque* clause. The Eastern Church, however, has continued to maintain belief in a single procession. We have not yet heard the end of the controversy, for in this ecumenical age some in the West think that we should go back to the original form of the creed, and the East stands firm by its position. Though I naturally lean to the Western view myself, I would be glad to see some compromise such as 'from the Father through the Son'. But let me now point out the implications for spirituality of the two points of view.

The Western view insists that the Spirit must be understood in the closest relation to the Son. Christ is the one in whom the Spirit dwelt in fulness, he is the one who went out from himself to the point of emptying himself, and, in accord with the paradox of the spiritual life, he is the one who manifests a full, mature, spiritual humanity. Hence the spirit of Christ and the Holy Spirit are scarcely distinguishable, and indeed they were not distinguished among some of the earliest Christians.

The advantage of this way of looking at the matter is that the Spirit and spirituality are interpreted in thoroughly christo-centric terms. The Holy Spirit is understood concretely in terms of Christ as the unique bearer and embodiment of that Spirit, and the goals of spirituality are set in terms of the Christ who has transcended to a new level of spiritual existence. Our Lord's teaching that 'God is Spirit' is inseparable from his own revelation of God; and likewise the consequence he draws that 'those who worship him must worship in spirit and truth' is inseparable from his own self-offering to the Father as the highest mode of spiritual worship and the spiritual life. Men are spiritualized, so to speak, to the extent that they become capable of following Christ in a self-outpouring of love and obedience. It is this that deepens and confirms them in their spiritual being.

On the other hand, the Eastern doctrine of a single procession has the advantage that it draws attention to something which, though not denied in the Western doctrine, has become overshadowed – namely, the relation of the Spirit to all creation. Dale Moody comments: 'Western theology has tended to confine the activity of the Creator Spirit to the redemptive realm of the Church, but Eastern Orthodoxy has vigorously challenged this confinement, and contended for both a creative and a redemptive work of the Spirit. At least on this point, the West can learn from the East, for creation cannot be excluded as a realm in which the Spirit works.'[16]

The whole creation is the domain of the Spirit. In the creation story, the Holy Spirit is associated with the Father and the Logos in the creative work. In the beginning, 'the Spirit of God was moving over the face of the waters'.[17] Some modern translations have 'wind of God' rather than 'Spirit of God' as a rendering of the Hebrew, but this makes little difference, for what may have at first been understood literally as a wind blowing over the face of the chaotic deep was interpreted in later times as the Creator Spirit, bringing shape and unity into the creation. Though we can only speculate on what the action of the Spirit might be on the lower or inanimate levels of creation, must we not interpret this too in analogy with his action on human spirits? This would mean that just as he brings men out of themselves, making them spiritual as he is himself Spirit, so he is breaking open those lower levels of creation in order to bring forth their potentialities for fuller development. Such a breaking open and bringing forth would be the theological equivalent of what in the empirical sciences is called 'evolution', the unfolding of the rich possibilities of nature.

But we are chiefly interested for the present in the question about the consequences for spirituality of this association of the Spirit with all creation. The point here is that, just as spirit belongs to all men, so the working of the Holy Spirit is not confined to the Church or even to the religious community in the broadest sense but may operate powerfully beyond its borders. It has been a major concern in the earlier chapters of this book to show that Christian prayer and spirituality have their secular counterparts outside of the Christian community. Surely Christians must gladly recognize that the Holy Spirit may work in very unexpected places, outside of the 'normal channels'. The Church is certainly the community of the Spirit, but it is not the exclusive field of the Spirit's working. Here again the ancient metaphor of the wind, as a clue to the meaning of 'spirit', is fruitful. 'The wind blows where it will.'[18] The wind cannot be channelled along set courses, and refuses to be shut up within limits. Likewise the divine Spirit cannot be restricted to narrow limits. The entire creation is the domain of the Spirit, and also the whole of time and history. No single community of persons, no particular geographical area or race of human beings, no specially privileged century or epoch can claim the Spirit for itself alone.

One might even come to believe that the more men attempt to restrict the operation of the Spirit to what they take to be the 'approved' channels, ecclesiastical or traditional, the more vigorously the same Spirit will manifest himself outside of these channels. The contemporary churches seem to get themselves increasingly involved in bureaucracy and look less and less like the community of the Spirit. It is hard to believe that they provide an ideal medium through which the Spirit can work, though neither can they exclude him. The Church has always needed its share of rebels and 'far out' people to save it from a legalism and institutionalism that can be deadening and unspiritual. It has needed also the stimulus of writers, artists and philosophers who, though not themselves Christians, have been voices through which the Spirit can speak to the churches and, indeed, to all men and women.

But while it is important to remind ourselves that the work of the Holy Spirit is as wide as creation and that aspiration to spirituality is as wide as humanity, we would certainly be wrong if we supposed that the Spirit is quite arbitrary in his working, or that we would be most likely to attain to the fulness of a spiritual existence if we were to turn our backs altogether on structures and institutions. That has been the mistake of the enthusiasts and fanatics of all ages, our own included. We have seen that the life of the spirit is indeed an 'ecstatic' life, but not in the bad sense of a disordered existence, swayed by irrational emotions and uncritical enthusiasms.

The Church is the community of the Spirit not in the sense of having a monopoly of the Spirit or of having the Spirit in its possession, but in the very real sense of having been called into existence by God, and having entrusted to it the Word and Sacraments. In the beginning, the Spirit had brooded over the creation. At Christ's baptism, the Spirit had descended in fulness upon our Lord. At Pentecost, the same Spirit was poured out on the Church. Those three events form a series which teaches us what is meant by calling the Church 'the community of the Spirit'. This expression does not refer to an exclusive characteristic of the Church, but asserts that in the Church there is going on in a concentrated manner that work of the Spirit which, in a more diffuse way, is also going cn throughout the whole creation. The Church is – at least, ideally – the growing point where the upbuilding work of the Spirit proceeds most intensely. We ought to be able to see in the Church a true spirituality, that process of breaking open and bringing forth the new qualities of a truly spiritual humanity. The Church, as community of the Spirit, should be the environment for the developing of full personhood. However imperfectly, the Church should be already exhibiting the eschatological kingdom of God, that final community of the Spirit toward which not only the Church but all creation is headed.

But there is still more to be said about the Church and spirituality. However difficult the road to spiritual maturity may be, we have all met some individuals who have made some progress along it and who are able to come out of themselves and give themselves in ways that often surprise us. Such individuals restore our faith, both in human nature and in the reality of the Spirit's work among us. But it is an important objection to traditional spirituality that it has been largely conceived in individualistic terms. Much of life nowadays is determined not by the actions of individuals but of groups, and often of large groups. The measure of spiritual achievement which we sometimes see in individuals seems to be impossible for groups. If, with difficulty and practice and divine grace, an individual may learn to go out from himself in a truly spiritual way, it seems that groups remain hard, self-regarding, unspiritual, unable to break out beyond their narrowly conceived interests. We have only to think of the social conflicts that surround us today between, say, unions and employers or between different racial and ethnic groups, to realize how self-regarding and unspiritual the life of society really is. Is this a situation that can never be changed, so that even if spirituality represents a possibility in the lives of individuals, social morality will always be a matter of power politics? I suppose that if one is realistic, one must acknowledge that groups will rarely give up any power or privilege unless forced to do so. But surely Christian spirituality envisages a broader strategy than the spiritualization of the individual. In calling the Church 'the community of the Spirit', we are implying that here there is a *corporate spiritual entity*, a society with the capacity to go out from itself. It has been said that the Church is the only society which exists primarily for the benefit of the non-member. To be sure, the Church has been often just as defensive, self-regarding and unspiritual as any other group. But whenever and wherever it is learning to be truly the Church, the community of the Spirit, it is introducing a new dimension into the social situation, one that gives hope for an eventual transformation.

V

Subjectivity and Objectivity in Theology and Worship

Christian theology has to do with the unfolding and elucidation of the knowledge of God that is given to us in the revelation in Jesus Christ. This knowledge of God is quite obviously a unique kind of knowledge. On the one hand, it is different from the knowledge of things. We get to know things through our senses and, in more sophisticated ways, through scientific investigation of the natural world; but God is not another thing that can be perceived by the senses, and none of the natural sciences discovers God as a phenomenon within the world. God is not a thing or an objectifiable phenomenon of any sort, but comes before all things as the condition that there may be anything whatsoever. On the other hand, the knowledge of God is also different from the knowledge that we have of ourselves. We get to know ourselves through the direct experience of being alive in the world, and from looking into our own minds and reflecting on what we observe there. We learn about ourselves too from our relations with other people who share with us the human condition. What we get to know in these ways is certainly very different from what we get to know when we look out on the world of things, and one might well agree that the personal inner life of man is closer to the mystery of God and affords a better glimpse into that mystery. Yet once more we are bound to say that what we know subjectively of ourselves is not God – and this applies also to what may be called the intersubjective knowledge that arises in our relations with other people. The life that we know within ourselves and in other human beings is finite, fragmentary, fallible, often torn by conflicts and stained by sin. It is not adorable and it is not God. Even an idealized humanity is not God, though it might be Godlike. Just as he comes before all things, so he comes before all finite persons. As the world of natural phenomena cannot contain him, so neither our subjective nor our intersubjective experience can contain him, for God transcends both the world and ourselves, and confers being on all.

Strictly speaking, then, we must say that the knowledge of God cannot be described either as objective or as subjective, for it transcends and precedes the distinction between them. God comes before every object and every subject, he is the encompassing, in the language of Jaspers. It is he who makes it possible for there to be objects or subjects at all, and so he himself cannot be included either in what we know as object or in what we know subjectively. God is not an object that we can describe in the same dispassionate way in which a botanist might describe a rare plant or an astronomer some celestial phenomenon. It would be arrogance to talk of God in such a way, as if he were just another phenomenon or another hypothesis, to be grasped and analysed by our minds. We know God only because he lets himself be known, and therefore our knowledge of him is not the mastering, objectifying knowledge that is characteristic of the natural sciences, but is a knowledge suffused with reverence and gratitude. The knowledge of God is inseparable from the adoration of God. Even when God did in the incarnation show himself among the phenomena of space and time, he was not directly perceptible, as an object presented to men's senses. Most people did not see God in Jesus Christ at all, and when St Peter, first among the disciples, did see into the depth of our Lord's being and confessed him to be the Messiah, the Son of the living God, he was told: 'Flesh and blood has not revealed this to you, but my Father who is in heaven.'[1] But while God is not to be grasped as an object that appears in the world, we would be equally in error if we thought that we could lay hold upon him within our own minds. Perhaps, indeed, the greatest arrogance of all would be to claim that if we cannot find God 'out there', then he must be 'in here', and some contemporary writers on theology seem to have come near to this error.[2] But although we find in our own minds and in the minds of others aspirations for the good, ideals of righteousness and justice, thoughts of perfection, the love of peace, none of these projections nor the sum of them can be called 'God'. They are all infected with our own limitations and sinfulness, and the reality of God far transcends them. Instead of putting these human ideals in the place of God, we need to lay our highest subjective and intersubjective aspirations before him so that they may be exposed to his judgment and purified from the self-centredness that clings to even the finest things of man.

To put it bluntly, it is idolatry to think that we have ever grasped God, that we have comprehended him either as an objective fact 'out there' or as an exalted ideal 'in here'. In all such cases, we are trying to take God into our possession. But this is just impossible (as well as being blasphemous). God transcends anything we can grasp or contain, and when we think we have him, the truth is that he has slipped through our grasp and we are left clinging to some pitiable idol of our own making. We can never know God by seeking to grasp and manipulate him, but only by letting him grasp us. We know him not by taking him into our possession (which is absurd) but by letting ourselves be possessed by him, by becoming open to his infinite being which is within us and above us and around us.

Thus the knowledge of God transcends both subjective and objective, and encompasses both. This unique kind of knowledge is perhaps at its highest and most intense pitch of awareness in silent adoration before the presence of God. 'Transported with the view, I'm lost in wonder, love and praise.'[3] Yet, because we are rational and social beings, we must speak of our experiences in order to communicate them, explore them and criticize them. Theology tries to put into words the knowledge that God has given of himself. But our human language is an imperfect instrument for expressing this unique knowledge of God, for as soon as we begin to speak we are bound to use language forms that belong to our everyday experience, whether objective or subjective, and that fall short of this unique encompassing experience of the reality of God. As theologians have known for centuries, nothing we say in words about God reaches to the fulness of his being, but we may be pointed to it indirectly. So the problem in theology becomes that of finding a language properly balanced or dialectical in which to speak of God – a language in which our subjective and objective ways of speaking must be combined and held in tension with each other, so that we are pointed to the unique Being who comes before all subjects and objects and cannot be reduced either to the one or the other. Well-known as an example of this tension in the history of theology has been the rivalry between objective and subjective theories of the atonement. Purely objective theories of atonement, like those that speak in terms of substitutionary punishment, tended to become impersonal and even subhuman – they were about a 'transaction' out there; purely subjective theories that dwelt on moral influence tended to become mere sentimental exhortations, reducing the action of God in Christ to a concrete illustration of the noble impulses already present in our own minds. Because God's reconciling work in atonement transcends both the subjective and the objective, we have to combine and bring into interaction these ways of speaking if we are even to glimpse the greatness of what God has done in Christ.

The trouble is that at different epochs in its history, theology is guilty of allowing its language to become onesided. The unique reality of God gets lost, and sometimes he is allowed to degenerate in our thought into one object among others in the world, while sometimes he is dissolved into our subjective ideals and imaginings. I think there can be no doubt that in the second half of the twentieth century the threat has come mainly from the side of an excessive subjectivism. In an analysis of the theological ferment of our times, Alec Vidler claims with justice that 'subjectivism and individualism' have been among its most obvious characteristics.[4] Of course, this subjectivism has been carried to the extremes of distortion among those theologians who have dispensed with God or proclaimed his death, and who have substituted for him their own subjective ideals. I am inclined to agree with T. F. Torrance's brusque comment that 'the root problem of the "new theologians" would seem to lie in the fact that they are unable to distinguish God from their own swollen subjectivity'.[5]

The trend toward subjectivism in theology has been in evidence for a long time, and its recent extreme manifestations only bring to unambiguous expression ideas which have been taking shape for many decades. Some would trace the beginnings of a onesided subjectivism to the theology of Schleiermacher, and certainly he did have influence on Feuerbach. In the twentieth century itself, it seems to me that some measure of blame can be laid at the door of most of the leading theologians. Although Karl Barth specifically criticized Schleiermacher and protested against the type of liberal theology which turned God into a kind of patron who might lend respectability to human aspirations, his general assault on 'religion' as a projection of the human mind has backfired. Barth wanted to except the Christian revelation from Feuerbach's critique of religion, but this critique had been specially directed against Christianity. Barth wished to assign objectivity to the biblical revelation alone, but without any natural or rational theology to support it, it was only too easy for the revelation to go the way of religion and be swallowed up in subjectivity. This is what actually happened among those 'new theologians' who had been in many cases followers of Barth before they gave up belief in a divine revelation. Rudolf Bultmann too had his share in encouraging the move toward subjectivism, for although he was careful to insist that existence is an encounter with a real other and that the aim of demythologizing is to uncover a veritable word of God, it was inevitable that some would interpret him to mean that God has been internalized in human experience and may be completely demythologized in terms of that experience. One may add the name of Dietrich Bonhoeffer as another influential Christian thinker who, whatever his own intentions may have been (and they remain obscure), has been appropriated by the subjectivizers. Among other things, they have seized on his idea that the practice of Christian faith should become more and more a 'secret discipline', without those outward manifestations or practices that had belonged to it in the past.

In the theology of our time, then, subjectivism is on the upswing. Perhaps it was necessary that there should be a move in this direction, and it probably has helped to make faith more lively and personal for many people. I have myself a high esteem for much of the work of the theologians named in the last paragraph. But when subjectivism reaches its extreme pitch and the objective elements in Christian faith are abandoned altogether, then, as I see it, the duty of the sane theologian is to hold the line and to stress the objective elements in Christian faith in the face of the subjectivizing flood. To do this, it will be above all necessary for him to strive to make known the reality and presence of

God, who embraces both the subjective and the objective, who cannot be confined in either and who sets limits to the presumptions of both.

Up till now I have been talking of theology, but the time has come for me to introduce the connection between theology and worship. To be sure, this has already been once or twice in view, as when I said that the knowledge of God is inseparable from the adoration of God and that perhaps the highest knowledge of God comes in silent communion with him. But now we must pay closer attention to the question of theology's relation to worship. When we try to give theological expression to the knowledge of God, we must keep in closest touch with the ways in which he makes himself known to the worshipping community, and this will be found to constitute our great safeguard against a false subjectivism. The dictum *Lex orandi lex credendi* contains a profound truth, for a genuine theology is shaped by the living knowledge of God in prayer and worship. Such a theology transcends the subjective-objective disjunction, and draws its contributions from both sides of the divide. Yet we must also think of the relation between theology and worship as a reciprocal one, for if worship shapes theology, it must in turn be subjected to the reflective criticism which theological thought engenders.

The recent forms of subjectivism, rooted as they are in the theologies of Barth, Bultmann and Bonhoeffer, have all one thing in common. They think of God's presence and approach to man almost exclusively in terms of the word of preaching. This has always been a basic weakness of Protestantism. The stress has been on preaching, instruction, hearing, understanding, that is to say, on what goes on in our minds. There is a kind of docetism in all this, as if we were almost disembodied spiritual beings, so that everything of which the Gospel speaks, finally God himself, has to be drawn into our minds. This intellectualism (perhaps better called conceptualism) leads toward subjectivism. Though I have mentioned especially the Protestant tradition, the preoccupation with the conceptual has characterized the Western attitude as a whole for several centuries, though sometimes – as perhaps now – there are movements of revolt against it. [6] The older tradition of Catholicism, on the other hand, has stressed the Sacraments rather than the Word. Its appeal is to the senses rather than the mind. It represents the pre-Gutenberg mentality and, if McLuhan is correct, also the emerging post-Gutenberg mentality of the age of television and electric immediacy. In this Catholic tradition there was the recognition that man is an embodied creature of flesh and blood, that Christianity is the religion of incarnation, that we learn through our senses as well as through our minds. The whole aim of the sacramental life is not so much instruction as incorporation, and this in turn fights against all individualism and subjectivism and teaches appreciation for the objective substance of the faith.

Of course, here again we are sometimes faced with extremes where there should be none. In the Middle Ages, the objectivity of the Sacraments was overstressed. They became so separated both from the Word and from the appropriation of the believer that distortion took place. But at the present time, with the overwhelming drift toward subjectivism, a new stress on the Sacraments is needed, and especially on the physical objective aspects of sacramental action and sacramental devotion. This could be a healthy corrective to the subjectivizing tendencies, and it could be all the more effective for not being presented in the form of *theological ideas* but in the *liturgical life* of the Church – a life which, as we have seen, exerts a powerful influence on theology.

Among the Sacraments, the Holy Eucharist has a pre-eminent place. In a remarkable way, it holds together Word and Sacrament in a unity, and so to give to the Eucharist a central place is to choose a basis which already militates against a damaging onesidedness. Current liturgical renewal has in fact paid special attention to the place of the ministry of the Word within the context of the Eucharist and has tried to secure that the meaningless rivalry between Word and Sacrament that has sometimes been the theme of polemics in the past is replaced by a better understanding of their essential complementarity. But, more than this, the Eucharist more than any other Sacrament or act of worship asserts the real objective presence of God in our midst. God was in Christ, and Christ, in turn, is in the Sacrament of his Body and Blood. Without denying other modes of presence whereby God and Christ are present to the faithful, we may none the less assert that the Eucharist is peculiarly the Sacrament of presence and confronts us with this presence in

physical objective realities.[7] Hence its importance in this age of
theological subjectivism run riot. Those who stress the place of
the Eucharist today are thereby stressing the objective reality
and action of God himself, and of his grace and judgment.

While we may be thankful for much in the liturgical movement of recent decades, especially for everything that gives the
Eucharist a more central place in the Church's life and encourages more intelligent participation in it, there are some innovations that should not be accepted uncritically until we have
fully examined their significance.[8] We have seen that while
worship can influence theology, the relation is a reciprocal one.
There can be little doubt that subjectivist theology has influenced some of the liturgical innovations of recent years. I am,
for instance, unable to share the enthusiasm of some people for
having the celebrant face the people during the Eucharist. I can
understand that it is good that all can see the manual acts at the
consecration. It is good too that there should be a sense of community between celebrant and people as they make Eucharist
together, and possibly this sense is heightened when they face
each other. On the other hand, I think Martin Thornton is
correct in judging that when the celebrant faces the people we
have a more subjective interpretation of the Eucharist and that
this could be disastrous without some compensating objectivity.[9]
That objectivity was, of course, stressed and even overstressed
when, in the Eastward position, celebrant and people as a
united body faced the altar of God. I shall not dogmatize about
this question, on which there are differences of opinion and good
arguments on both sides. I have wondered whether the old-
fashioned Anglican custom of celebrating at the north end may
have something to be said for it after all, as it makes the best of
both worlds! If, however, the Westward position comes to be
more commonly adopted, there must be found some way of
ensuring the recognition of the mystery of God's objective presence to his people, otherwise it may all degenerate into an
exercise in subjectivity or intersubjectivity. I should certainly
think that some parts of the eucharistic liturgy – for instance,
acts of confession and the declaration of faith in the reciting of
the creed – call for the Eastward position, as united acts by
celebrant and people before God. In any case, it is only in the
alternation of the Eastward and Westward positions that either

of them has any psychological significance in worship. Either of them in isolation would become flat and meaningless.

But this has been something of a digression. The Eucharist has undergone many changes in the course of Christian history and will no doubt undergo many more. In spite of all – or because of all – it has remained the great focus of Christian devotion to a Power not ourselves, an objective Reality who yet impinges on the innermost core of our lives. The place and value of eucharistic worship were never more important in the Church than they are today, when the whole fabric of Christian faith is being subjected to so many strains and uncertainties. Those who work to ensure that the Holy Eucharist shall be the main occasion of Christian worship; those who encourage due reverence in the preparing for and receiving of the Sacrament; those who seek to have the Blessed Sacrament as the focus of Christ's presence in every church – those who do these things are not only following a proved and valuable tradition of Christian devotion but are witnessing and responding to the needs of today in affirming the objective reality of God.[10]

VI

Theology and Spirituality

Theology and spirituality appear to present a contrast. Theology
is an intellectual discipline, and many of its practitioners have
claimed for it the name of 'science'. Spirituality, on the other
hand, is a seeking for a quality of life, and as such it appears to
be more concerned with the feelings and the will. Now it has
become almost a dogma in the Western world that any study
which may rightly claim to be a science must be purged from
the influences of feeling and will. It must be 'value-free', to use
the expression that has been current among philosophers. It
must deal in facts that are objective and universally accessible,
and it must rigorously exclude all subjective evaluations which
might prevent us from seeing the facts as they really are 'in
themselves'.

This theory about the value-free character of science has
raised problems for those who devote themselves to theology.
Some have been persuaded that because theology implies some
faith-commitment and because in the past it has often been
closely intertwined with the spiritual life, with prayer, worship,
belief and so on, it must surrender the claim to be a science or an
intellectual discipline. Others have tried hard to divorce theology from religious involvement, so as to make it – as they
suppose – intellectually respectable. They have tried to develop
a purely academic or scientific theology, a neutral study of the
phenomena of religious faith, and they have claimed that this
scientific theology can take its place in the universities alongside
the secular sciences.

I do not believe that one need be driven to either of these

positions. Both of them tacitly assume the dogma of the value-free character of science, and I happen to think that this dogma is false. Every science, every intellectual discipline, involves its practitioners in a form of spirituality, in valuations, aspirations and commitments. These take different forms in different sciences, and sometimes they are more plainly exhibited than at other times. Yet something of the sort is always present.

In saying this, I do not for a moment believe that my remarks tend in the slightest degree toward anti-intellectualism. On the contrary, I would agree that anti-intellectualism constitutes a very grave danger to a human and humane society. This needs to be stressed in these days, because there is undoubtedly a reaction against the too rigid and too narrow exaltation of intellect that has been a feature of Western culture in the past few centuries, and there is the danger, as I have readily admitted,[1] that this reaction could become a flood which might sweep us (and has already swept some) into fanaticism, superstition, sentimentalism and just plain mindlessness. One of the most sympathetic interpreters of the current revolt of many American youths against the values of a society in which science and technology have reigned supreme, Theodore Roszak, has compared their spiritual questings to the chaotic upsurge of religiosity and superstition in the Hellenistic world. He writes: 'In the turgid floodtime of discovery, sampling and restive fascination, perhaps it would be too much to expect disciplined order of the young in their pursuit.' Yet he sees hope in what may eventually come from the revolt against a too narrow rationalism. He goes on to say: 'It is quite impossible any longer to ignore the fact that our conception of intellect has been narrowed disastrously by the prevailing assumption, especially in the academies, that the life of the spirit is a lunatic fringe best left to artists and visionaries . . . an antiquated vocabulary still used by the clergy, but intelligently soft-pedalled by its more "enlightened" members.'[2]

No, the alternative to a narrow value-free intellectualism is not anti-intellectualism. If I seek to relate theology to spirituality, then it must not be in that illicit way against which Paul Tillich once warned when he counselled theologians not 'to fill in logical gaps with devotional material'.[3] To do that would be anti-spiritual as well as anti-intellectual; for intellect belongs inalienably to spirit, yet spirit is a wider reality than intellect alone.

To explore the relation of theology to spirituality, we shall explore some facets of the theological task, and, as each of these is examined, we shall find that it has a dimension that leads into spirituality. But we shall find that at several points one could say something similar about the secular sciences.

We begin with the claim that theology is an intellectual discipline. As the very name 'theology' indicates, this is *logos*, rational discourse concerning a given area of subject-matter, and therefore part of the whole intellectual enterprise of mankind. Several times already in this chapter I have used the expression 'intellectual discipline'. This is a very common expression, but we rarely pause to consider just what it means. The various sciences and studies in which men engage are rightly called 'disciplines' because those who pursue them must submit themselves to observe certain rules and principles. Although we are thinking chiefly of theology, what I am saying at this point holds for every science and study which can claim the name of 'discipline'. Every science has its standards of integrity, and whoever would pursue that science and attain proficiency in it has not only to abide by those standards but has to accept them, internalize them, absorb them into his own nature as a person. We use the expression 'intellectual honesty'. To be a scientist, a philosopher, a theologian, an historian or whatever it may be, one must implicitly commit oneself to the ideal of intellectual honesty. For in pursuing any serious study, one takes upon himself the responsibility of uttering the *logos*; the *logos* in turn, by its very nature as assertion, claims to be an unveiling of truth; and whoever would seek truth and speak truth has taken upon himself moral obligations.

To say that because the sciences pursue truth to the exclusion of personal feelings and prejudices they are therefore value-free seems to me to betray a gross misunderstanding. The man who lets truth guide his mind and who is docile to the given is a man who takes value, including moral value, very seriously indeed. We have already noted that the sciences are called 'disiciplines'. We might go further and say that every serious study implies its own asceticism. It is not for nothing that we commonly say that someone is 'devoting' himself to his studies. This language of devotion is basically a religious language. He who devotes himself to his science gives himself up to it, he denies himself in subjecting his own prejudices to the evidences and in subordinating his desires and pleasures to the pursuit of the truth on which he has set his mind. And, of course, this holds even if he does not speak of anything so grandiose as 'the truth', for in most sciences one can hardly hope for more than approximations to the truth.

All sciences, I say, have their ascetic aspect, and this is once more reflected in our ordinary language, for we speak of the 'rigour' of science and of its 'strictness'. Theology, like other intellectual disciplines, has its own asceticism. The study of theology is, in fact, inseparable from a kind of mortification. It is always painful to surrender prejudices and cherished beliefs, but it is most painful of all when these prejudices touch on matters that concern our lives most deeply, so that the loss of them seems at the time to threaten us with the collapse of our world. Is there anyone who has studied theology and has not found it sometimes to be a painful pursuit? Convictions that we have held for a long time without questioning may be found, when we subject them to theological scrutiny, to be untenable. Unless we have experienced this kind of intellectual mortification, and unless we go on experiencing it, I doubt if we have ever been much in earnest with theology. One of my Glasgow students once came to me after a lecture and said, 'In five minutes you have shattered the beliefs of a lifetime.' I tried to explain to him that it had not been my intention to be destructive and also that for a young person like himself there was presumably still quite a slice of his lifetime left in which some new theological construction might take place! But I also pointed out to him that the initial confrontation with theology can hardly be anything other than a shattering experience, as our private beliefs, long unquestioned, are set against the given and subjected to critical scrutiny. Furthermore, there will continue to be some shattering as long as one pursues the theological path. For theology is more than the mastering of propositions and the manipulation of concepts. It is an intellectual quest, *fides quaerens intellectum*. Like all intellectual quests, it commits the inquirer to a discipline of intellectual honesty and integrity, and it may well be that it is in theology that this discipline is experienced in its sharpest and most painful ascetic character, for theology deals with those convictions which are very near the heart of human existence. These are the convictions about which we are emotionally involved at the deepest level, and about which honesty can be achieved only through a rigorous spiritual discipline.

T. F. Torrance has well expressed the situation of the theologian in these words: 'Objectivity in theological science, like objectivity in every true science, is achieved through rigorous correlation of thought with its proper object, and the self-renunciation, repentance and change of mind which it involves.'[4] Torrance here uses the expression 'object' where I have preferred to speak of the given, but his meaning seems to be much the same. He makes a distinction between 'objective' thought which takes its form from that which is thought about, and 'objectifying' thought which (in the case of theology) turns God into a manipulable object.

It may be asked, however, whether the theologian can hope to practise the kind of discipline we find in other sciences. These other sciences, or at least some of them, have fairly definite methods, and the integrity of the scientist consists in his faithfulness to these methods and his rigorous application of tests such as might verify or falsify any hypothesis under consideration. In the case of theology, it is sometimes said that its assertions are incapable of verification or falsification. This raises very large questions which cannot be adequately discussed in the present context.[5] But I think it will be enough for the present to say that Christian theology includes *some* empirical assertions which are susceptible to the kind of tests mentioned. I have in mind especially historical assertions, as, for instance, the assertion in the Apostles' Creed that Jesus Christ 'suffered under Pontius Pilate, was crucified, dead and buried'. In principle, this assertion is as capable of verification or falsification as any other assertion about the past. For a long time now, theologians have recognized that if they are to maintain intellectual integrity, then the historical assertions of Christian faith must be investigated by the same methods that the secular historian employs in his investigation of the past. This has led to the rise of historical criticism of the Bible and so eventually to a vastly changed attitude toward the Bible. This new attitude has been attained only after long disputes and much pain, and it is maintained only at the cost of a continuing vulnerability. Yet, in accepting the risks inherent in historical criticism, theology has been strengthened – certainly not weakened, as some suppose. If in recent decades the conceptual structure of theology has been thrown into some disorder by the questions arising out of historical criticism, the inner discipline of the subject has been immeasurably strengthened. For theologians have made it clear that they are prepared in their inquiries to share the same risks as attend those who pursue other sciences, and to submit themselves to the same kind of *askesis*, perhaps even in an eminent degree.

It may be useful at this point to make explicit a distinction which has already been implied in some of the foregoing remarks – the distinction between conceptualism and intellectualism. Conceptualism has an eye to logical structures; it is concerned with the results (including the provisional results) of inquiry rather than with the inquiry itself; it is, generally speaking, static and impersonal. By contrast, intellectualism is concerned rather with the actual process of knowing, and understands this as a process that is dynamic, personal and governed by its own inherent standards of integrity. Conceptualism easily consorts with the idea of a value-free science on the one hand and with an immutable dogmatic theology on the other; it understands truth as a property belonging to propositions in abstraction. Intellectualism on the other hand considers truth primarily as the value governing the drive for knowledge; and whereas conceptualism tends toward positivism, intellectualism is open toward mystery, for the dynamic drive of the intellect continually presses beyond what has been conceptually grasped.

The youth revolt of today and the counter culture which it is seeking to build is, I think, better understood as anti-conceptualist than as anti-intellectualist. To be sure, the youth itself does not pause to make this distinction, and the distinction has not been clearly made in the Western tradition of the past few centuries. Academia has come to be regarded as the precinct of the value-free, the neutral, the non-involved. But it would be a pity if it came to be supposed that the only alternative to this is the emotive, the immediate, the partisan. As against this false disjunction, there needs to be developed the notion of a dynamic intellectualism which can provide a sane vantage-point amid the conflicts of interest, not because it is value-free but precisely because it is deeply committed to the most compelling values of all – in other words, because it is an intellectual quest allied with a spiritual discipline.[6] Such an intellectualism is the ally of the current revolt against the established order, and without a firm intellectual basis, the revolt will degenerate into triviality. Perhaps theology can have some part in commending to our time the ideal of an intellectualism which is at the same time value-committed.

In most of the foregoing discussion, we have been thinking chiefly about characteristics which theology shares with all intellectual disciplines. But each science or discipline has its own distinguishing features, arising from its special subject-matter and from the methods which it devises for studying this subject-matter. We shall now attend more closely to the special characteristics of theology, though we shall find that some of these too have their counterparts in other disciplines. We shall consider how these special characteristics fill out the notion of a spiritual discipline, accompanying theology and contributing to it.

First among the special characteristics of theology should be mentioned the fact that theology is the work of the Church, the product of the community of faith. Actually, many disciplines have now developed a communal character. The individual investigator of earlier times has been replaced by the team, working co-operatively. And even beyond that, one would have to recognize nowadays a kind of community of science to which each scientist gives a tacit allegiance. 'Submission to intellectual standards, 'writes Polanyi, 'will be seen to imply participation in a society which accepts the cultural obligation to serve these standards.'[7] Yet I think it may be said that theology is *par excellence* a communal work. It has always been true that theology is the work of the whole Church and brings to expression the faith of the people of God. The word 'heretic' means the pure individualist, the man who disregards the community for the sake of his own likes and dislikes. I deliberately use the expression 'likes and dislikes' here, for in genuine heresy, the discipline of thought has been abandoned. Heresy (which is probably very rare) is not to be confused with experimental thinking. On the other hand, it does not follow that the theologian must be a conformist. Far from it. Within the community (but not in disregard of it) he has his own function as one who is charged with reflection on the meaning and implications of faith, and if he reflects in accordance with those principles of integrity of which we have already spoken, and reflects *for the community and with the community*, then his reflection will sometimes cause pain and tension in the community as well as in his own mind. Theology has its prophetic and critical dimensions, and part of the theologian's work is to help the community to see, as well as to let his own seeing be opened up by the insights of the community. The most irenic theologian is bound to have some collisions with views that are circulating in the community and even dominant in it. But finally the theologian has no existence apart from the community.

It is not surprising that so much first-class theology has come out of the religious orders. Men reading the office together, sharing in eucharistic fellowship, contributing to and drawing upon a common life, have an extraordinarily rich resource for theological work. Admittedly, there has always been the danger that such a community becomes too narrow, and no one can deny that the history of theology has been plagued with factionalism. Today, however, theology has become one of the most striking manifestations of a genuine ecumenism, and fruitful exchanges are taking place among different traditions without destroying the integrity of these traditions. The Christian theologian has, in a new way, become responsible to the whole people of God – and he is increasingly aware that ideally the people of God embraces all mankind.

What I am saying then is that the study of theology teaches the discipline of the common life. The very doing of theology demands that one become open to a community – first, perhaps, a limited community in seminary or religious order or chapter or faculty; beyond that, to an historical community that has persisted through many changes; beyond that still, to the wider multitudes of mankind who are seeking to become a community, a genuine people. Theology both demands and fosters the spirit of community; its business is not just to speak, but to know when to listen and when to interpret, when to speak and when to be silent. Truth is not just an abstraction to be attained by intellectual effort. Truth requires also that we are true to each other. This is a discipline of the spirit, sometimes hard and occasionally painful, for it demands honesty as well as charity, 'speaking the truth in love'.[8]

A second peculiarity of theology has to do with its unique subject-matter. Theology has to do with God, with the unconditioned, the ultimate. If it is Christian theology, it has to do with God in Christ. All sciences do not conform to the same pattern. Each one is to some extent shaped by its particular subject-matter. Some sciences can be more or less purely objectifying in their approach. Such, for instance, would seem to be physics and chemistry. History, on the other hand, is an example of a science whose practitioners have to participate to some degree in the kinds of events and phenomena which they describe. They need sympathy, experience, understanding, imagination, in order to interpret these events. Theology is more like history in this regard than it is to physics, and yet theology seems to make even greater demands on those who take it up. For what would it mean to study God in Christ? I have acknowledged already that Christian theology, in so far as it makes or implies historical assertions, is concerned with establishing facts, and to that extent it must accept the secular historian's discipline of scientific investigation of the facts, and it must be docile in face of them. But this is only a beginning. Theology goes on to that sympathetic imaginative interpretation of the facts, such as the historian also employs in his attempt to interpret the phenomena of history. But theology does not halt even there, for the claim of Christian faith is that *God* was in Christ, that something of ultimate import has come to expression here. This is what makes theology altogether unique among the disciplines. The subject-matter of Christian theology, God in Christ, is not a passive object laid out for our scrutiny, not even another human reality to be met in terms of reciprocity, but the transcendent reality which already encompasses us. To put it in another way, if Jesus Christ is the *logos*, then the peculiarity of Christian theology is that this discipline is *logos* concerning *logos* itself.[9] Or again, if Jesus Christ is, as he claimed to be, the truth, truth in living personal form, then theology is the seeking of truth concerning truth itself.

So we can observe a steady deepening of the discipline as we consider the theological quest for truth. The quest involves us first in the discipline of being true to ourselves, of maintaining intellectual honesty and integrity; it involves us next in the discipline of being true to the neighbour, in the openness and reciprocity of our common quest for truth; it involves us finally in being true to truth, to that living truth that is already there ahead of us and that we could not find unless it drew us to itself. Certainly, when we use the name 'God', one thing we must mean by that name is truth, the final reality that is uncovered when all illusions and errors have been stripped away. The desire for truth implanted in us is the desire to know the real, and 'God' is our name for that which is most real. The desire for truth is the desire for God. St Augustine wrote: 'Where I found truth, there found I my God, who is the truth itself. And thus since the time I learned thee, thou abidest in my memory; and there do I find thee whensoever I call thee to remembrance, and delight in thee.'[10] We should not fail to notice how in these sentences Augustine slips quite naturally from theology to prayer, from third-person language in which he talks *about* truth and God to second-person language in which he talks directly *to* God as the truth. Is this an illustration of that illegitimate practice against which Tillich warned, of filling in the logical gaps with devotional material? Assuredly not. For if the final truth of the world is not something dead or something merely material but the truth of a living, spiritual reality, a personal reality, even a suprapersonal reality, then the quest for that truth can end only in the communing with the truth, and it is this communing which we call prayer.

Let me illustrate this point further by drawing attention to one other peculiarity of theology – its method. To be sure, this is a complex matter. There is more than one theological method and we have seen already that the method of theology cannot exclude the ascertainment of empirical facts. But when one comes to the deepest and most significant problems of theology, the method is that of meditation, letting the mind become immersed in the concepts, symbols, teachings, dogmas, stories of the Christian faith. Philosophers too know this kind of meditation. The celebrated phenomenological method, worked out by Husserl and his followers, has obvious resemblances to the spiritual discipline of the mystics and involves a clearing of the mind from illusion and prejudice so that it may be exposed to 'the things themselves'. Another philosopher, F. H. Bradley, wrote of metaphysics, 'the intellectual effort to understand the universe', as 'a principal way for some persons of experiencing Deity'.[11] Intellect and prayer are not opposed to one another. On the contrary, some of the highest forms of intellectual endeavour bring us to a style of meditative thinking not far removed from the kind of prayer which masters of the spiritual life have practised for many centuries.

Theology and spirituality are two paths by which men seek God. On first glance, they look like very different paths, but finally they converge. Spirituality proceeds by way of prayer, worship, discipline. By these means, men have transcended themselves, their personal being has been enhanced and they have known communion with God. Theology, on the other hand, proceeds by way of intellectual inquiry. It accepts the rigour of a commitment to intellectual honesty. Yet those who pursue the way of theology find that this too is a discipline drawing them beyond themselves. They are drawn to a Truth which is no dead truth to be locked up in propositions or stored away in a book, but a living Truth, self-communicating and itself the source of all truth. A dynamic theology does not cease to be a scientific discipline because it is inspired by the passion of an intellectual love. It cannot rest content with a knowledge *about* God and it positively abhors a chattering about God. Knowledge of God, like knowledge of our friends, must finally be a knowledge based on communing. The knowledge of God merges with the love of God.[12]

VII

Eucharistic Theology and Liturgical Renewal

The Eucharist sums up in itself Christian worship, experience and theology in an amazing richness. It seems to include everything. It combines Word and Sacrament; its appeal is to spirit and to sense; it brings together the sacrifice of Calvary and the presence of the risen Christ; it is communion with God and communion with man; it covers the whole gamut of religious moods and emotions. Again, it teaches the doctrine of creation, as the bread, the wine and ourselves are brought to God; the doctrine of atonement, for these gifts have to be broken in order that they may be perfected; the doctrine of salvation, for the Eucharist has to do with incorporation into Christ and the sanctification of human life; above all, the doctrine of incarnation, for it is no distant God whom Christians worship but one who has made himself accessible in the world. The Eucharist also gathers up in itself the meaning of the Church; its whole action implies and sets forth our mutual interdependence in the body of Christ; it unites us with the Church of the past and even, through its paschal overtones, with the first people of God, Israel; and it points to the eschatological consummation of the kingdom of God, as an anticipation of the heavenly banquet. Comprehensive though this description is, it is likely that I have missed something out, for the Eucharist seems to be inexhaustible.

But the very denseness of the Eucharist, the weight of meaning and experience concentrated in it, gives rise to a problem. All the items that I have mentioned are interconnected and interdependent, and to lose any one of them would mean an impoverishment of the whole and eventually a distortion of all the other items. The problem then is to present the Eucharist in such a way that its wholeness will not be broken and that we shall not be cut off from any of the resources which it brings. To say this, however, is not to deny that at different times and in varying cultural situations, different items from the Eucharist will have special stress laid upon them. While the basic structure of the Eucharist has remained constant, it has received widely different expressions in East and West, in the early centuries and in modern times. This diversity of expression and of emphasis is not only legitimate but necessary if the Eucharist is to remain alive and to meet the needs of the changing generations. One cannot have very much sympathy with the group of prominent English agnostics and humanists who joined in a petition to Pope Paul VI for the retention of the Latin mass in its traditional form. They were concerned with the Eucharist as a contribution (and certainly a notable one) to 'civilization' rather than as an act of living worship. These cultured patrons of religion are perhaps no less dangerous than the cultured despisers of Schleiermacher's time. But it would have been a legitimate ground for protest if it could have been shown that some vital eucharistic truth was being suppressed, and this is always the danger in liturgical renewal. Such renewal is necessary if the Eucharist is to remain alive. Also, such renewal inevitably brings changes of emphasis, so that what was formerly prominent may be pushed into the background, and what was formerly scarcely noticed may now acquire new importance. But the point is that such changes of emphasis have to take place *within the whole eucharistic context* or else we get misleading half truths. A Jesuit writer, Herbert Francis Smith, begins an article on this theme as follows: 'The mass is a meal taken together by the people of God. To say this is true, but to say this and to say no more is to say less than nothing, for it is to say something misleading.'[1]

It is therefore the very fulness of the Eucharist that makes its presentation in an adequate way so difficult. The ideal might be to let everything be launched upon us simultaneously. According to Marshall McLuhan, Western man is moving out of the 'linear' type of mentality, in which one pays attention successively to one item at a time, to a kind of holistic mentality appropriate to the age of electric immediacy. He tells us: 'We are suddenly eager to have things and people declare their being totally.'[2] We hear of experimental theatres where people now watch two or more plays at once (though Americans have for long been addicted to the three-ring circus). Experimental forms of worship have been devised where all sorts of things go on at once – a film being shown, *loud* music being played, a meditation being read – so that the worshipper is bombarded at several points simultaneously. The fulness of the Eucharist invites comparison with these contemporary forms, and even the traditional eucharistic celebrations were very much of the multi-media kind. In a High Mass, for instance, many things go on at once – words are being uttered, music is being played, there are lights, vestments, ceremonial acts, the worshipper himself has his appropriate gestures to make; and in addition to what is seen and heard and understood, there may also be the smell of incense and the taste of bread and wine. It is very much a total experience. One is, so to speak, assailed through every channel of mind and sense. One's whole being is enveloped in the eucharistic action, and perhaps this is how it should be if the Eucharist is meant to transform and sanctify human life in its entirety.

But, in spite of McLuhan, most people still retain something of the linear mentality. They find that they have to attend to one main thing at a time, and complain of getting a headache if asked to absorb too much all at once! So the problem of liturgy arises, or part of the problem: in what order is the Eucharist most effectively presented? How, for instance, does one begin – with a confession of sin or a shout of praise or what? Even to ask this question makes it clear that there is no ideal liturgy, for answers will always vary. While it may be possible to devise an ecumenical liturgy that could be used by large numbers of Christians on special occasions, such a liturgy would be a somewhat colourless affair, and on ordinary occasions of worship it is likely that a wide variety of liturgies will continue to be used, catering for the many varieties of human needs and temperaments. A plurality of liturgies and a plurality of emphases is legitimate, provided that none of them actually deny any essential element in the Eucharist as a whole.

For several decades now what is broadly called 'the liturgical

movement' has been at work and its fruits have been appearing
in the large crop of new liturgies which have appeared in many
communions and denominations, Roman, Anglican and Protestant. On the whole, this has led to a considerable revitalizing
of eucharistic worship. On the other hand, it was inevitable that
there should be errors and exaggerations. In some cases, the
aims of the pioneers of the liturgical movement have been
realized. In other cases, these pioneers themselves have been
disillusioned by the direction which events have taken. The
liturgical movement cannot be viewed simply with uncritical
enthusiasm. Nevertheless, it seems to me that certain gains have
been made, and from these there can be no turning back. These
gains are to be found in almost all the new liturgies that have
proliferated in recent years, so that they constitute, as it were, a
kind of family, resulting from modern liturgical research. Let
me mention four such gains.

1. The new liturgies give a fuller and more distinctive place
to the ministry of the Word.[3] This is done by providing a fuller
lectionary, including the possibility of more lessons from the Old
Testament as well as readings from the Epistles and Gospels. The
giving of a sermon or homily at all celebrations is encouraged,
this coming immediately after the Gospel so that it is obviously a
'preaching of the Gospel'. This appropriately puts the Nicene
Creed at the end of this whole section as the people's response
of faith to the hearing of the Word. The history of Christian
worship, especially since the Reformation, has been bedevilled
by a false rivalry between Word and Sacrament, and by the
neglect of one for the sake of the other. The new liturgies aim at
the ideal of a full ministry of the Word within the context of
sacramental worship, and if the aim is fulfilled, there will be as
a result an immensely strengthened people of God.

2. The new liturgies are at pains to restore in a clear and un-
mistakable way what Gregory Dix called the 'fourfold shape' of
the eucharistic action. 'For in the night in which he was be-
trayed, he *took* bread; and when he *had given thanks* to thee, he
broke it, and *gave* it to his disciples.' Of course, this fourfold act
of taking, giving thanks, breaking, giving had always been there
in the traditional liturgies, but its shape had become blurred.
The Latin rite before Vatican II, for instance, in spite of its
great antiquity and its many beauties, was repetitious and long-

winded. The rites of the Anglican Prayer Book had quantities of material, mostly penitential, inserted between the moments of the eucharistic action. As Mark Gibbard has well expressed it, it is rather as if in these traditional liturgies a beautiful well-proportioned room had had all kinds of furniture and adornments brought into it (all very beautiful in themselves) until it became cluttered up so that the original proportions were hard to discern. Generally speaking, in the new rites the four moments of offertory, consecration, fraction and distribution follow one another without clutter and yet without hurry, and this is a great gain in making clear what the heart of the Eucharist is.

3. By encouraging the participation in the Eucharist of all the people of God, the new rites make clearer the corporate nature of the Church and its worship. There are no spectators at the Eucharist – we are all engaged in it. Yet the fact that we are a body means that we do not all do the same things. The life of the body is an ordered life, and each order, whether bishops, presbyters, deacons or lay people, has its distinctive function to perform. This is genuine 'concelebration' in the fullest sense of the term, each making his distinctive contribution to the total action. No doubt Rome had further to go than most other Christian communions in this matter of encouraging the participation of the people, in view of such customs as non-communicating High Masses and the practice of saying private devotions during mass. But all groups tended to make the people mere spectators and have benefited from the new awareness of the corporate character of the Eucharist and so of the Church itself. For the Church manifests its true nature in the concelebration of the Eucharist. In Gabriel Moran's words, 'the Eucharist is the Church at her best.'[4]

4. I think I would add as another gain the flexibility of the new liturgies, which allow for alternatives, even for alternative canons. There is something to be said for a middle ground between the rigidity of an absolutely fixed liturgical form and the absence of fixed forms altogether. There should be a stable recognizable structure, but this is quite consistent with the provision of alternative usages and wordings suitable for special groups, such as young people, or suitable for different types of congregations.

The four matters mentioned I have recognized as gains, and

I think many people would agree with this assessment. But there are other matters that are more debatable, and something has to be said about them.

It may be asked first of all whether liturgical reformers have not been too much influenced by historical criteria. It is true that certain norms were given in the early practice of the Church and in the New Testament, but it is a mistake to assume that what can be shown to be more primitive must be liturgically better. As Gregory Dix has said, the meaning and wording of the Eucharist 'were left to the Church to find for itself, and there was nothing to suggest that this was a process to be completed by the first Christian generation'.[5] Those liturgiologists who do make the appeal to the early history of the liturgy are in any case divided among themselves, for while some want to take the first century as the model, others are willing to go down to the end of the first five hundred years. One occasionally suspects that the secret prejudices of his own century may colour the liturgical reformer's preference for this or that primitive norm. We may remember that nineteenth-century New Testament scholars tried to get back to what they supposed to have been the original Gospel, though when we now read their works we can see that they understand this Gospel very much in terms of the moral and political ideals of their own epoch. The contemporary student of liturgy must be careful that he does not fall into the same kind of mistake. How, for instance, can one account for the recent popularity of the liturgy of Hippolytus, except on the grounds that it happens to combine a fairly early date with features that are congenial to some contemporary ecclesiastics? The liturgy itself is undistinguished, and concerning Hippolytus my predecessor F. L. Cross has remarked that he was a 'reactionary' and 'not a master of his subject'.[6] I wish to assert as strongly as possible that any liturgical practice or formula is to be judged in terms of theology and spirituality, and that nothing is to be either approved or rejected because it happens to be in its origin first century or late medieval or nineteenth-century or even twentieth-century! One may hope that through all centuries the Holy Spirit leads the Church into an understanding of truth, on liturgy as on other matters.

The historical forms have to be related to the cultural patterns of our own time, and the liturgical reformers have been much concerned about this. Our own age is more humanistic in its outlook than most of the earlier periods of Christian history. In particular, greater stress is laid on human dignity, and it is not supposed that in order to glorify God man must, as it were, grovel in the dust. I am in hearty agreement with this, and the point has been made several times already in this book. The new attitude is reflected in the new liturgies. The excessively penitential mood of the older liturgies has been modified, and there is stress instead on joy and thankfulness. If the new liturgies seem somewhat Pelagian by older standards, I do not think this is altogether a fault. It becomes a fault only if penitence is altogether excluded, and if that happens, then I believe the joy too must be diminished, for how can man truly rejoice unless he has heard the words, 'Your sins are forgiven!'? What was wrong with the older liturgies was not their inclusion of a penitential moment but their constant harping on penitence and unworthiness. What would be wrong in the new liturgies would be such a violent reaction against the penitential mood that an act of penitence and absolution is either omitted or quickly 'got out of the way' at the beginning. There is much to be said for placing such an act immediately before the offertory, as a preparation of the people corresponding to the preparation of the gifts.

The other side to this problem is the Godward reference of the liturgy. The older liturgies stressed the majesty and transcendence of God, and the Eucharist was typically considered as an offering to God. The newer liturgies de-emphasize these aspects, and call attention rather to that aspect of the Eucharist in which we think of it as a holy meal and a human fellowship. This correction certainly needed to be made in the Roman communion. But there is some validity to the complaint that the correction has been made in such a heavy-handed manner that the dimension of mystery and transcendence is in danger of being lost altogether and the Eucharist reduced to triviality. Let me quote three recent comments to this effect, one Roman, one Anglican and one Reformed: Schillebeeckx, 'Prayer in interaction with one's fellow men is a deeply Christian reality, but it is cut off from its true source if it is not accompanied by moments of purely passive communion with God. If the modern tendency toward "horizontalized" Christianity ignores this essential element, then in its heart it will have cut itself off from the Christianity of Christ';[7] the Archbishop of Canterbury, 'It is urgently necessary to show that what is offered in the Eucharist is the stuff and substance of daily existence as it is . . . but the wise liturgical reformer will not let this concern for the relation of the rite to the secular blind him (as sometimes happens) to the otherworldly and supernatural aspects of the sacrament';[8] Allan D. Galloway, 'If the sacrament of Holy Communion becomes assimilated to the common meal, it is in danger of becoming no more than a common meal. But at the same time, to deny all relationship between it and the bread of the market place would be to deny its power as sacrament.'[9] This united testimony from such a broad spectrum is impressive, and deserves to be heeded. We must notice that each of the three quotations recognizes that there are two truths to be satisfied and is only concerned to criticize those oversimplified solutions which omit or grossly underrate one of the truths.

I believe that appropriate ceremonial can go far toward bringing together the horizontal and vertical aspects of the liturgy. The traditional ceremonial had become too fussy and complicated and, like the fourfold action itself, needed to be streamlined so that its meaning could become clear. But there should still be one great moment of oblation and adoration in which the human fellowship is offered in union with Christ to the Father. In a contemporary celebration with the consecration *adversus populum*, this climactic moment seems to come best at the doxology ending the canon when, at the words 'all honour and glory', host and chalice are lifted up together before the people in recognition that all comes from God and is offered to God. Incidentally, this used to be called misleadingly the 'Little Elevation', though in fact it was 'the proper and primitive elevation'[10] long before the separate elevations at the words of institution were introduced in the thirteenth century. But in view of what has been said earlier, it will be clear that I am recommending this practice not because it is primitive but because of its theological and spiritual appropriateness.

The new liturgies must also be expected to fulfil certain aesthetic demands. Obviously one can hardly ask for immortal prose, but at least there should be freedom from verbiage and good cleancut English with enough rhythm to make it suitable for reading aloud or even for singing. Masters of liturgical language are probably very rare indeed. English did have one in Cranmer, and it seems to me that in the Anglican communion at least, the most successful attempts at a revised eucharistic liturgy have been those which have rearranged the order and modified the theology in accordance with modern principles but have stayed as far as possible with Cranmer's language. This has also helped to maintain a sense of continuity between the new rites and the old, making it clear that whatever changes may have been made, there is one Church and one Eucharist throughout the ages. Thus, even if some of the language has an archaic flavour, this is not a fault. There is in any case no language, even the most up-to-date, that would convey an instant understanding of the Eucharist or would take away the need for long instruction in its meaning.

One point that arises in this connection is the question whether God should be addressed as 'Thou' or 'You'. It is incorrect to say that 'Thou' is obsolete in this usage – it has until recently been current usage in prayer and liturgy, though obsolete in addressing other persons. There is a certain advantage in using the 'Thou' language with respect to God, because it stresses the unique reality of God. He is not just another person to be addressed like the rest. This was brought home to me forcibly some time ago in conversation with a radical young priest who had problems with the traditional doctrine of God (or the traditional image of God) but certainly believed in God as the unique adorable mystery to be addressed by the unique pronoun reserved to Deity, Thou.

Thus while we must be grateful for many things that have come out of the liturgical movement, others have to be viewed more critically. The quest for a liturgy both catholic and contemporary is not easy to satisfy. As indicated above, the theological and spiritual criteria must be paramount, but they are not separable from others. Eucharistic theology needs to be embodied in a rite related both to the historical sources and the prevailing cultural conditions, and finding expression in an appropriate language.

VIII

Eucharistic Presence

Though the Eucharist contains in itself many meanings, all of them essential, there is nevertheless one which seems to be fundamental. This is the meaning of presence. In this Sacrament, Jesus Christ is in a unique way really present with his people.

Presence is a most important category both in theology and in spirituality. But the word 'presence' has several different significations. For a beginning, it may be helpful if we think of some of the kinds of presence that we know in daily experience, and go on from these familiar instances or models to consider the mystery of eucharistic presence.

In ordinary usage, we seem to talk of presence in three main ways. First, there is temporal presence, or presence now. This kind of presence is opposed both to the past, which is no longer, and to the future, which is not yet. The presence of a pain, for instance, means that I am feeling it now, though perhaps I was not feeling it yesterday and will not be feeling it tomorrow. Next, there is spatial or local presence. This is presence here, and is opposed to distance. That which is locally or spatially present is near me or beside me. The presence of butterflies in my garden means that they are congregated in this spot. Thirdly, there is also personal presence. When one person is present to another, this is more than their contiguity in space. Latin had a special preposition to express the notion of personal presence: *coram*. To be *coram vobis* is to be in your presence; to be *coram Deo* is to be in the presence of God. This notion of personal presence is more difficult to define than either temporal presence or local presence. It usually includes temporal and local presence, presence here and now, but perhaps not always. For instance, the friend who is at the other end of the telephone line is personally present, though locally absent. But personal presence implies communication or communion, a meeting of persons, and this is much more than the juxtaposition of objects in space or their contemporaneity at a moment of time. Let us keep these three modes of presence in mind for further use as we go along.

Meanwhile, let us think of another distinction relevant to our discussion. This is the distinction between particularity and universality. When we talk of someone or something being present, we seem to be pointing to something quite particular, to a here and now that contrast with a region from which the person or thing is absent. If someone or something were present everywhere and all the time, would it make sense to talk of 'presence'? Now God is believed to be universally present, and presumably Christ, as the divine Logos or Second Person of the Trinity, is also present at all times and in all places. But how can this be reconciled with the idea of a particular presence – with the doctrine of the incarnation, for instance, according to which God was present in a particular way at a particular time in a particular place? Perhaps it could be said that the particular presences of the Logos are made possible by his universal presence, and obviously the Lutheran doctrine of consubstantiation made considerable use of the notion of ubiquity in its attempt to talk of eucharistic presence. But it is very important not to let particular presences be simply swallowed up in a universal presence. I doubt very much whether such a universal presence could ever be detected or recognized unless we were pointed to it by particular presences – moments of intensity, of meeting or encounter. It is part of our human nature to seek those particular occasions. In the Old Testament, as the understanding of God deepens, he is seen more and more to be God of all the earth and not merely of one nation or one territory. Yet the people always sought some particular place or time where God might be known in his definiteness. The ark of the covenant, the tabernacle, the temple, the cloud or *shekinah*, these were, shall we say, focalizing centres where the presence was experienced with peculiar intensity.

Let us now return to our three models of presence. All of them have had a place in the history of Christian worship.

As far as the temporal presence, presence now, is concerned, the Church has known various ways in which Christ is represented or made present again. The Council of Trent, incidentally, used the word *repraesentatio* in connection with the Eucharist in the sense that it makes present again Christ's saving work. We live between the Christ of history, of the historical incarnation, and the Christ of the future, the Christ who will come again with glory. But 'between the times' Christ is not absent. He is present to us in many ways. One important way is the proclaiming of the Word. It is Christ's living Word to us and he is present in it. This has been stressed by many modern theologians, especially those associated in one way or another with kerygmatic theology. Bultmann practically identifies the living voice of preaching with the Easter faith in the present living Lord.[1] Ian Henderson said about Bultmann that he recognizes a 'real presence' in preaching.[2] I would myself hesitate to use the expression '*real* presence'. I think Bultmann certainly recognizes a *genuine* presence in preaching, but when one uses the adjective 'real', is there not an allusion to its derivation from Latin *res*, 'thing', so that a real presence is in some sense a thingly, physical or embodied presence? It is this that Bultmann lacks, and so does Protestant thought in general, for the Eucharist itself tends to be understood as merely *verbum visibile*. Bultmann explicitly says of Christ that 'he meets us in the word of preaching and nowhere else'.[3] This absurd limitation of Christ's presence to the sermon must be rejected out of hand. Christ is present now in the preached word, but in many other ways besides.

Local or spatial presence has been very important in Christian worship also. There are holy places, and shrines and churches have been set apart. I am not much impressed by some current criticisms of church buildings. We all know very well that the building itself is not the Church, and that God is not confined to sacred buildings but may well be conducting his principal business outside of them. But one has again to ask the question whether presence can be recognized in the broad undistinguished stretches of the world if there are no focal points where we can become sensitive to its quality. If there were no oases in the secular desert to remind us, could we ever attain to the thought of all life informed by Christ? Hugh Montefiore has expressed the matter very well: 'We need a symbol of the sacred in the midst of the secular to remind us that all is sacred and that we all have souls. The church is a symbol of celebration and joy and leisure and privacy, a sign of transcendence, a pointer of silence and tranquillity; a church is sacred space, symbolizing to us the sacredness of all space.'[4] If there were no particular places where one might find Christ present, I do not think he would be present anywhere.

I move on to the personal model, which seems to me the mode of presence which should be normative for the interpretation of the Eucharist. We should notice first of all that personal presence is not a merely spiritual presence, for a person is embodied and includes a physical presence. Normally, when another person is present to us, we not only hear him but may see him and even touch him. Even the presence of God we may think of as mediated through some this-worldly realities. Buber, in his famous book *I and Thou*, suggests that every meeting with another finite 'thou' can be the vehicle for a glimpse through to the eternal 'Thou'. It seems that even an inanimate object can be encountered in such a way as to afford a glimpse of a reality beyond itself. Buber speaks of encountering a tree not merely as object or botanical specimen or instance of natural law but as quasi-personal presence, in some kind of sacramental sense.[5]

The ways by which Christ's presence communicates itself in the Eucharist are manifold. It is a multidimensional presence, not to be reduced to a moment of time or a point in space, but more like that broadly embracing if less easily definable type of presence that we call personal presence. The eucharistic presence includes that word-presence which we have already considered in connection with preaching, for the reading and proclaiming of the Gospel form a normal element within the Eucharist. Then there is also the action or drama of the Eucharist, and Christ is present in that, for it is *his* action. He is present also in the community of the faithful, which is the body of Christ, sometimes even called the 'extension of the incarnation'. We must also say that Christ is present in the bishop or president of the Eucharist, for Christ is himself the High Priest and our human *sacerdotium* is a sharing in his priesthood. As a writer in *Sacramentum Mundi* has expressed it, Christ is himself *minister principalis* of the Eucharist, its veritable president. The many dimensions of Christ's presence in the Eucharist warn us against trying to fix too precisely a 'moment of consecration' or an exactly delimited *locale* of presence, for personal presence cannot be restricted within the models of temporal and spatial presence. Yet, on the other hand, personal presence is no simply spiritual and still less diffuse presence, and in detailing the multidimensional character of Christ's personal presence in the Eucharist, we may be in some danger of lapsing into a vagueness concerning this presence.

Therefore we have now to come to the crux of the matter and assert that, within the total context already described, Christ is present *par excellence* in the consecrated bread and wine. This is the centre of eucharistic presence. He took bread, and said, 'This is my body'; and likewise wine, saying, 'This is my blood.' In his great study of eucharistic origins, Jeremias has demonstrated that these words of Jesus can refer only to the bread and the wine – not, as is sometimes said, to the action or to the community.[6] In the Eucharist, Christ's body, his embodied presence is above all to be identified with the consecrated elements. Here indeed we come to a *real* presence, if we take this word 'real' in its traditional sense. A real presence is not simply a genuine presence, but an embodied, even a thingly presence. The Word is not merely heard and understood but really made flesh, so that we can say 'we have heard, we have seen with our eyes, we have looked upon and touched with our hands.'[7]

I have said above that of the three types of presence which we know in ordinary experience, personal presence has a normative role in the interpretation of what we mean by eucharistic presence. It seems to me that this is where contemporary views of eucharistic presence will differ from some of the older views, both Catholic and Protestant. Among Protestants who have believed in a genuine presence, this has usually been conceived as a spiritual presence, but a spiritual presence is less than a personal presence, for, in contemporary understanding, a person is embodied. Catholic views were also something less than fully personal, for they stressed spatial or local presence and tended to isolate the consecrated elements from the context of community and action. Thus they tended to visualize presence as location in the elements, or again, in respect of time, they made much of a 'becoming' present, a dramatic moment of consecration. Now the concept of personal presence when applied to the Eucharist does not deny that these other ways of understanding the matter have their share of truth – far from it. There cannot be a truly personal presence without, in some sense, a spiritual presence, a spatial or local presence and a temporal presence. But the concept of personal presence gathers up these fragmented understandings into a more inclusive understanding, and in doing so it passes beyond some of the narrower limitations of the traditional views. Presence, understood as personal presence, is indeed focussed in the consecrated elements as its centre, but it is not restricted to them. Likewise, there is no precise moment of consecration. The whole prayer of consecration consecrates, so that a single elevation at the end of the prayer seems more appropriate than separate elevations at the words 'This is my body' and 'This is my blood'.[8] And yet, within the context of the action, the community, eventually the whole Christian history, the consecrated bread and wine become for us in a real sense our ark, our tabernacle, our temple, our *shekinah*, the particular meeting place where, having met Christ face to face, we can go out and perceive him in a thousand other places as well.

Let me turn to the difficult subject of theories of presence. All personal presence has some mystery in it, and cannot be reduced simply to an empirical phenomenon. Therefore no theory of eucharistic presence can ever be more than an approximation. I am sure there are many people who devoutly believe in a real presence and are content not to seek any theory of it, perhaps even believing that such theories can be divisive. At the same time, I do not believe that we can avoid the obligation of theological inquiry. The Christian has a duty to understand, as far as he can, the meaning of his faith. And this is no luxury but has many practical consequences. Only someone who has tried to understand the meaning of eucharistic presence can defend it in a world too prone to regard it as a mere superstitious survival. Or again, in the whole vexed matter of intercommunion among different groups of Christians, I do not think there can be meaningful intercommunion at any depth – I am not talking about shallow exercises in politeness – unless there is some clarity about eucharistic doctrine. We cannot all do something together unless we have at least some common understanding of what we are seeking to do.

So we cannot shirk the question about a theory of eucharistic presence. In the Western Church, as we all know, the doctrine of transubstantiation held sway for a long time. In many ways, that theory had much to commend it. It ruled out all magical theories of presence, though the irony is that both in popular piety and among critics of the theory, this was not understood. Thus one still reads in reputable reference books that what happened at the so-called 'miracle' of Bolsena was that a priest who entertained doubts about the truth of the doctrine of transubstantiation had these doubts resolved when, during the celebration of mass, he saw blood flowing from the consecrated elements. If he had seen such a phenomenon, then it ought not to have convinced him of the truth of transubstantiation, for on the contrary it would have proved the utter falsity of that doctrine. For the doctrine maintains that there is no change in the accidents and so there can be no bleeding hosts or any such pseudomarvels. According to this particular theory of eucharistic presence, there is no discernible difference in the elements whatsoever before and after consecration. Physics and chemistry have got nothing to do with what happens in consecration; or, to put it in different language, one could never get any empirical verification of the presence of Christ in the consecrated elements. There being no empirical verification, the presence is visible only to the eye of faith. It is perceptible only to that eye that sees things in a depth beyond the physico-chemical. As St Thomas puts it: *Praestet fides supplementum sensuum defectui*.

But this theory of transubstantiation has been under attack for a long time. In spite of what has been said in the last paragraph, it did all seem too magical and superstitious to the Reformers. At a later time, even more serious damage was done to the theory by the philosophical critique of the category of substance, and I would have to say myself that I would have great difficulty in working with the category of substance as traditionally understood. But I think that most recently the inadequancy of the theory of transubstantiation has been seen to lie in its preoccupation with the spatio-temporal models of presence rather than with the personal model. That is to say, of the three models which I have described above, transubstantiation is concerned primarily with a presence understood as presence at a particular time in a particular place, whereas my own argument has been that the notion of presence that is of paramount importance for eucharistic theology is the personal presence of Christ among his people.

Some Roman Catholic theologians have now become dissatisfied with the traditional doctrine of transubstantiation and we have heard a good deal of the doctrine of transignification. This doctrine has been elaborated by a number of scholars, mostly Dutch and of whom P. Schoonenberg has been one of the most original. One should not think of transignification as a rival theory to transubstantiation or in any fundamental conflict with it. Rather, it is trying to say some of the things which transubstantiation failed to say. But a personal embodied presence certainly implies some form of spatio-temporal presence, whether this is to be understood under the category of substance or in some other way.

The doctrine of transignification uses as its interpretative categories not traditional notions like substance and accident but notions derived from modern phenomenology and existentialism. One could build a theory of transignification very well out of a chapter of Heidegger on 'The Worldhood of the World'.[9] There he discusses what is meant by a 'world', and shows that a personal human factor enters into any concept of world. A world is constituted by a nexus of significations and a whole universe of meaning is thereby built up. Things within the world are constituted not merely by substance (in fact, this category is not used in the philosophy under consideration) but also by signification, by the way they are incorporated into the personal, historical world of mankind. Everything gathers around itself an aura of meaning. If we come up against something that is utterly strange to use, we immediately begin to try to relate it to the whole field of meaning.

A world can be understood as a unified structure of meaning, and to belong in a world is to participate in such a structure of meaning. Some things have gathered round themselves quite a considerable aura of meaning because these things have had a special importance in the life of persons and in the history of mankind. This is readily understandable when we remember that a world has always, as one of its constitutive factors, a human and personal dimension. As an illustration, let us think for a moment of light. One may describe this in purely physical terms as waves or photons or the like. But this is an abstract way of thinking. In human experience, light is a rich symbol-laden phenomenon associated with life, goodness, beauty and so on. These symbolic connotations are not extra meanings that have simply got tacked on, so to speak, as if the bare physical concept were itself all that really matters. All of the meanings go to constitute the being of light, and I use the word 'being' advisedly. The various significations belong to the ontological structure of light.

Likewise, to bread and wine there belong many meanings or significations. Indeed, it would be difficult to think of either bread or wine in a purely physical way, as a mere natural phenomenon, for bread and wine are not products of nature alone, but of man's labour. Thus their very meaning (and so their very being) is related to the personal life of mankind. They already belong in a world that is shaped by persons. Now, 'transignification' – if I understand the theory correctly – indicates 'a change of meaning', 'a shift of meaning', perhaps even 'a new depth of meaning'. I find that there is some ambiguity in the use of the expression 'transignification' among Roman Catholic theologians. Sometimes it seems to indicate the transignification from Passover to Eucharist; the bread and wine which our Lord took within the context of the Passover meal he moves into an entirely new context – the context of the Eucharist. That was undoubtedly a remarkable and unique transition, which took place at the institution of the Eucharist. But more important perhaps for the theology of eucharistic presence is the transignification that takes place within the Eucharist itself – the transignification of the bread and wine as they receive the meaning of the body and blood of Christ. Joseph M. Powers expresses it thus: 'The realizing presence of Christ takes place through the fact that bread and wine become signs of him . . . what happens is a change in the sign-reality of the bread and wine.'[10] Now, let me say at once that this is not a subjectivist and still less a receptionist doctrine of the eucharistic presence. If we are going to make the personal model central in our attempts to construct a theory of eucharistic presence, then the distinction of subjective and objective becomes irrelevant and misleading.[11] In the case of a meeting of persons, the presence of one person to another cannot be described in terms of something merely there objectively. My friend is not there as an object over against me; he is there with me in a reciprocal relationship. This is the point of the *nobis* in the traditional Latin mass, in that part of the canon known as the *Quam oblationem: ut nobis corpus et sanguis fiat dilectissimi Filii tui Domini nostri Jesu Christi*, 'that it may become *for us* the body and blood of thy most beloved Son, Jesus Christ our Lord.' Almost the same words appear in Cranmer's Anglican rite of 1549, where God is asked to bless the 'creatures of bread and wine, that they may be *unto us* the body and blood of thy most dearly beloved Son, Jesus Christ.'[12] On the other hand, the denial of a sheer objective presence is not the assertion of subjectivism. If my friend is not there as mere object, neither is he there in my subjective imagination. There is undoubtedly a givenness about his presence. It seems to me that receptionist doctrines of eucharistic presence have been infected by a distorting kind of subjectivism. Such doctrines are not only inadequate but, I venture to say, presumptuous, as if Christ's presence somehow depended upon our faith letting him be there, and this surely puts the cart before the horse. The initiative is Christ's and he is, as we have said, the *minister principalis* of the Eucharist. He enables us to have faith and, indeed, to be persons capable of knowing his presence. Our personhood is not something we already possess, but something that comes into being in relation to other persons; and in the Eucharist above all our personhood is enhanced, even created, through the presence of the person of Christ. He is there before we are. Our presence to one another in the Eucharist, the so-called horizontal dimension, is made possible only through Christ's already being present and communing with us. He is present in and through the transignified elements; and though their meaning is *for us*, it is he, not we, who confers it. Meaning is not some sort of subjective colouring which we project on to things that are neutral in themselves. Meaning or signification belongs to the being of things, it constitutes them part of a world and so constitutes them in their thinghood or reality.

Personal presence is in no sense a denial of spatio-temporal presence but is a broader, more inclusive mode of presence and brings the whole question of eucharistic presence into a fuller context. One consequence of this is that the 'moment of consecration' ceases to stand out as a kind of isolated climax, while the actual communion and the meal aspect of the Eucharist acquire more importance. The shift of emphasis is obvious in contemporary liturgies. The theological background to this, whether or not it is always consciously understood, is the shift from spatio-temporal to personal models of presence. If this is understood, then I think the change of emphasis is justified. But if it is not understood, then there is the danger that the Eucharist becomes trivialized as a common meal and nothing more.[13] We must be careful not to fall into new distortions and to ensure that through appropriate words and ceremonial there is an unambiguous recognition of that real presence of Christ which at once judges and makes possible the presence to one another of the faithful.

I now proceed to somewhat more difficult matters, though these are not unrelated to the concern expressed at the end of the preceding paragraph. What happens to the consecrated elements at the end of the Eucharist? What people do with them is often a good guide to what theology of presence they hold, though they may hold this theology only in a subconscious way. If, for instance, the consecrated bread is thrown into the garbage receptacle and the consecrated wine poured down the sink, then there seems to be no belief in a *real* presence, though I would not rule out the possibility of belief in some genuine *spiritual* presence at some stage of the proceedings. However, if the elements are reverently consumed or reserved, such acts are capable of being construed as implying belief in a real and abiding presence. (There are other possibilities – I remember a Scottish minister who after the service of Holy Communion would pour what was left over of the wine on the graves in the churchyard.) In such cases the abiding presence is understood as still within the context of the Eucharist. This is also true in the case of taking the reserved sacrament to the sick – a very ancient practice which goes back to the time of St Justin at least.[14] But it needs to be said repeatedly in these matters that it does not matter very much when a particular practice came into currency. We do not decide the merits or demerits of such a practice on antiquarian grounds.

But what about the reservation of the sacrament in churches as a focus of devotion, a centre of the real presence? In this case also, one may say that the context of the liturgy is being extended and the eucharistic perspective enlarged.[15] We can see this very easily in the case of taking the reserved sacrament to the sick, but there is in principle no difference in the case of prayer and devotion before the reserved sacrament.

Indeed, such practices can be an important way of making that kind of extension that has to be made, whereby the liturgy enables us to see all life as sacramental. I would venture to say that these devotions have a special value at the present time, namely, that they teach us that sometimes there is the need for passivity before God. Here one has got to stand against the trend of the times and not conform to the fashion. That fashion is activism, but there are occasions when our action has to be suspended before Christ. Activists are in constant danger of becoming too intense, too politicized, too polarized, too self-righteous. I hope it does not sound frivolous to say: 'Relax a little in the presence of Christ!'

That presence, whether in the Eucharist itself or in some of the devotions that have grown out of it, is perhaps the most precious source of Christian spirituality. One can well understand the need that there has been to break out of individualism and pietism, and to stress the meal character of the Eucharist, its horizontal dimension and all the rest. But the indispensable foundation of it all is the real presence of Christ in his appointed sacrament.[16]

Eucharistic Sacrifice

In an earlier chapter, we considered the topic of eucharistic presence.[1] Now I would like to turn to another aspect of the Eucharist – the Eucharist as sacrifice. This has been a very controversial topic in the past, but I would like to defend the notion of eucharistic sacrifice, though in a form which, I hope, would be widely acceptable.

First of all, it is desirable to say something about sacrifice in general. Sacrifice is one of the most ancient of all religious acts, and also one of the most universal, having a place in both biblical and pagan religion. It is unfortunate that sacrifice has become so closely associated in the popular imagination with killing and the shedding of blood, for surely the essence of sacrifice lies in offering something to God, something that is of value in the eyes of the one who offers it. According to a leading authority on Greek religion, what sacrifice evinced was the recognition of a higher obligation than simply the need to satisfy one's own physical needs.[2] But this deeper and truly religious significance is obscured by the prevalence of such images as that of the sacrifice of animals to secure the favour of the gods. The modern mind turns away from such an image with horror, but we must not let this prejudice us against any understanding of sacrifice. We can still appreciate self-sacrifice – the offering of one's goods or even of one's life for the sake of another or of a cause or even of God. This is the kind of sacrifice that we must have in mind when we think of the sacrifice of Jesus Christ, whether on Calvary or in the Eucharist. It is something affirmative: Christ gives his life, so Christians believe, for the sake of the world. It must be admitted that when theologians have tried to explain just how Christ's death was (or is) a sacrifice and just how it effects salvation, they have not been able to agree. Some of them, in fact, have still been thinking in terms of ancient and frankly barbaric conceptions of sacrifice, perhaps as the appeasement of God's anger or as the punishment of a victim who takes our place. In any approach to the problem of eucharistic sacrifice, we must set aside such ideas. Certainly the word 'propitiation' should be avoided, since it so definitely suggests an enraged deity who has to be mollified. So we would find misleading the phrase of the Council of Trent which referred to the mass as a 'propitiatory sacrifice for the living and the dead'[3] and likewise the Anglican Prayer Book's use in the 'comfortable words' of the verse 'he is the propitiation for our sins' (I John 2.2). The Greek word translated 'propitiation' in the verse just quoted is *hilasmos*, which contemporary scholars translate by the vaguer term 'expiation' (RSV) or simply by the broad expression 'sacrifice' (Jerusalem Bible). This newer way of understanding the matter is far more affirmative, and has a more worthy conception of God, than the older ways, though these old misconceptions were used to stoke the fires of controversy.

However, much more than a matter of words was involved. At the time of the Reformation, probably most Protestants as well as Catholics thought of sacrifice as propitiatory. The difference was that Protestants believed that the uniqueness and adequacy of the sacrifice on Calvary was threatened if one allowed that the Eucharist too was in some sense a sacrifice. Cranmer went so far as to declare that the Roman Catholic teaching about eucharistic sacrifice is 'the greatest blasphemy ·and injury that there can be against Christ'.[4] Of course, it is probable that Cranmer and others misunderstood the Catholic teaching, or that they based their views on popular superstitions, or even that sometimes they deliberately caricatured the Roman view. At any rate, they represented the Roman Catholic view as holding that the mass is a repetition of the sacrifice of Calvary, and also that the more masses that were said, that is to say, the more repetitions that were made, the more benefits would be secured both for the living and the dead. Actually, these crude notions of repetition and of the quantitative virtue of many masses were not the true teaching of the Roman Catholic Church. When the doctrines of that Church were restated in the sixteenth century at the Council of Trent, the word used about the mass in relation to Calvary was not *repetitio* or 'repetition', but *repraesentatio*, 'representation', or (more literally) re-presentation, making present again. The sacrifice of Calvary is, in one sense, perhaps the primary sense, an event of world history which can be dated with reasonable accuracy to the month of April in the year 30 of our era, and as such an historical event, the sacrifice of Calvary is unique and unrepeatable. But Christians have attached such importance to that event that it has become for them more than a once-for-all happening in the past. There is no denial of the adequacy and finality of Calvary, but the claim is made that this event still touches the present and can be renewed in the present – it is 'represented and applied', in the words of Trent. The sacrifice of Calvary is not tied to a moment of time but touches all times. According to one New Testament writer, the [sacrificial] Lamb was 'slain from the foundation of the world' (Rev. 13.8). The text is admittedly obscure, but from it the philosopher Hegel and a host of theologians have drawn the theological truth that an act of self-giving or self-emptying is an eternal characteristic of God. From the beginning sacrifice was there in the mind and purpose of God and remains effective as God's unchanging purpose towards the human race. So it is believed that in the mystery of the sacrament, Christ's sacrifice is again present to the worshippers, though in a different manner, as it was to those who stood by Calvary.

If we cast our minds back to the beginnings of the Eucharist, we see that it was inevitable that sacrificial associations would attach themselves to this rite of the new covenant. First of all, what was it that Jesus and his disciples did in the upper room? Three out of the four Gospels, namely Matthew, Mark and Luke, tell us that the little band had met together to observe the Passover. John's Gospel has them meeting on the day before the Passover, but this still maintains the connection, and as it was on the day before the Passover that the sacrificial lambs were killed, the link with sacrifice is intensified rather than diminished.

The Passover itself was a sacrificial feast. The account of the institution of the Passover (Ex. 12) is likely to be ideal rather than historical, but it shows us how the Jews had for a very long period of their history understood what the rite was about. A lamb was to be taken and killed, and its blood exhibited on the lintel and doorposts of the house. So when the angel of the Lord came to slay the firstborn of the Egyptians, he would pass over the houses on which the blood of the sacrificed lambs was to be seen. This, it was believed, was the original Passover, and it was to be observed in all future years. 'You shall observe this rite as an ordinance for you and for your sons for ever,' says Moses. 'And when your children say to you, "What do you mean by this service?" you shall say, "It is the sacrifice of the Lord's Passover." ' According to this account, the blood of the sacrificed lambs procured deliverance for the Israelites. It was surely natural to see the new rite which arose out of Jesus' Last Supper with his disciples as the new equivalent of the old Passover, the sacrifice of the new covenant replacing the sacrifice of the old. Jesus' own death very soon came to be regarded in a sacrificial way – 'a ransom for many' (Mark 10.45). When he said at the meal, celebrated only a few hours before his death, 'This is my body, given for you,' and 'This is my blood, shed for you,' then whether or not that meal was formally a Passover meal, it certainly carried the associations of the Passover and could hardly fail to be eventually understood as a new Passover, in which Jesus himself is equated with the paschal Lamb.

According to Paul (our oldest written account of the Supper) and Luke, Jesus also said, 'Do this in remembrance of me', or, as Dom Gregory Dix translated, 'Do this for the recalling of me.' The Greek word translated 'remembrance' or 'recalling' is *anamnesis*, and scholars seem to be agreed that in such contexts this was a very strong word – not a mere remembering of the past as past, but more like Dix's 'recalling' or Trent's 'representing'. In the words of Jeremias's classic study of eucharistic origins, this kind of remembrance 'is never a simple remembrance of something but always an effecting and creating event'.[5] The 'agreed statement' on the Eucharist produced by the Anglican-Roman Catholic International Commission says this about it:

Christ's redeeming death and resurrection took place once

and for all in history. Christ's death on the cross, the cul-
mination of his whole life of obedience, was the one, perfect
and sufficient sacrifice for the sins of the world. There can be
no repetition of or addition to what was then accomplished
once for all by Christ. Any attempt to express a nexus between
the sacrifice of Christ and the eucharist must not obscure this
fundamental fact of the Christian faith. Yet God has given
the eucharist to his Church as a means through which the
atoning work of Christ on the cross is proclaimed and made
effective in the life of the Church. The notion of *memorial* as
understood in the Passover celebration at the time of Christ –
that is, the making effective of an event in the past – has
opened the way to a clearer understanding of the relationship between Christ's sacrifice and the eucharist. The eucharistic memorial is no mere calling to mind of a past event or
of its significance, but the Church's effectual proclamation
of God's mighty acts. Christ instituted the eucharist as a
memorial (*anamnesis*) of the totality of God's reconciling
action in him. In the eucharistic prayer, the Church continues to make a perpetual memorial of Christ's death, and
his members, united with God and one another, give thanks
for all his mercies, entreat the benefits of his passion on behalf
of the whole Church, participate in these benefits and enter
into the movement of his self-offering.[6]

Though I believe that this statement just quoted could be
clarified and improved at certain points, it does seem to me a
remarkably adequate account of what is essential in the notion
of eucharistic sacrifice, and we shall see later that it does indeed
bridge some differences that in the past seemed seriously
divisive as between Rome and Canterbury.

There is a further point to be noted here in support of the
sacrificial interpretation of the Eucharist. There is a measure of
ambiguity in that word *anamnesis*. Who is being reminded of the
sacrifice of Christ, who is being asked to recall it? Usually we
think of those who are celebrating the Eucharist, but are they
the only ones? Some scholars, including Jeremias, point out
that the Eucharist is a solemn recalling before God, so that
God too is being reminded, the saving death of the Son is being
pleaded before the Father. To quote some words of Geoffrey

Wainwright: 'The eucharist is a dominically instituted memorial rite which, not only serving to remind men but also being performed before God, is sacrificial, at least in so far as it recalls before God with thanksgiving that one sacrifice and prays fror the continuing benefits of that sacrifice to be granted to us now.'[7] Of course, it might be said that God does not need to be reminded of anything. But this rather obvious truth does not abolish the human psychology that longs for the full coming of the kingdom and in praying God for its coming, points to the work of Christ in its inauguraiton and continuing reality.

In what I have just been saying, I have been supporting the conception of a eucharistic sacrifice by appealing to ecumenically minded scholars in the Roman Catholic, Anglican and other traditions. Perhaps it could be objected that the case seems stronger than it is because I have cited modern writers who have been influenced by the ecumenical spirit, and Anglicans who have lived after the Oxford Movement and the Anglo-Catholic revival of the nineteenth century. But if we were to go back to the classical Anglicanism of the period, say, 1550–1850, was not the notion of eucharistic sacrifice consistently repudiated, as indeed we noted in the sentence I quoted from Cranmer? Are we not seeing now an artificial attempt to cover over cracks that lie very deep and among the several traditions? Certainly the older writers could not have expressed themselves in terms which today have become widely acceptable. But I believe that if we follow Cardinal Newman's advice and read Anglican documents in the most Catholic sense that they will bear (as he himself did in the well-known Tract 90) we shall find that what is essential to a doctrine of eucharistic sacrifice has never been abandoned by Anglicans, and that the Church of England's recovery of its Catholic inheritance was indeed a recovery, not an invention or a new departure. Though like all historical entities it has been subject to change, the Church of England claims that in essence it has through all the changes, including the English Reformation, remained true to that Catholic form of Christianity which was first brought to these shores.

Let us then look back for a few moments to Cranmer who, as we have seen, expressed himself so vehemently against the notion of eucharistic sacrifice. It has to be remembered that

Cranmer went through many stages in his career, beginning from mediaeval Catholicism and moving through something akin to Lutheranism to more extreme forms of Protestantism which, some scholars have maintained, came close to the views of Zwingli. No specially original or even unambiguous theological position comes to expression with Cranmer. Indeed, as Cyril Richardson brusquely expressed it, 'Cranmer was no philosopher and, as a theologian, he belongs only to the second rank.'[8] To this we have to add the further weakness noted by his biographer, Jasper Ridley, that 'belief in the royal supremacy became for Cranmer as fundamental a principle as his belief in the supremacy of scripture'.[9] So we need not look for anything very profound or penetrating in Cranmer, though perhaps some of his critics, especially Gregory Dix, have been too severe.

But Cranmer did have one redeeming virtue. His mind was stored with the traditional liturgical texts and he had a facility (never equalled since his time) for turning them into rhythmic and sonorous English. This proved to be providential for the Church of England and eventually for the Anglican Communion. What Cranmer personally believed or how he understood those liturgical texts is of slight importance, for the new English versions, like all written or printed texts, acquired in their public form an independence and objectivity which requires us to interpret them without having regard to the subjective views of their author. So in spite of what Cranmer said in his writings about the Eucharist, a doctrine of eucharistic sacrifice does unquestionably appear in the liturgical texts appointed for use in the Church of England at that time. It is of course the case that in the first Prayer Book of 1549 (and repeated in all subsequent editions of the Prayer Book) Cranmer included near the beginning of the Prayer of Consecration a clause intended to affirm the uniqueness of the sacrifice of Calvary: 'who made there (by his one oblation once offered) a full, perfect and sufficient sacrifice, oblation and satisfaction'. No one, Catholic or Protestant, could object to this clause, which has as its antecedent Jesus Christ, and we have seen that very similar words were vigorously affirmed in the 'agreed statement' of Anglicans and Roman Catholics in 1971. But as the prayer of 1549 continues, there follow other expressions taken from the old Latin liturgies, not conflicting with the words about the 'one oblation once offered' but capable, as we shall see, of yielding an adequate expression of eucharistic sacrifice. We find such expressions as the following: 'We thy humble servants do celebrate and make here before thy divine majesty with these thy holy gifts, the memorial thy Son hath willed us to make' (and the word *memorial* here is to be taken in the strong sense of *anamnesis*, as we have seen); then we come to the well-known phrase, 'entirely desiring thy fatherly goodness mercifully to accept this our sacrifice of praise and thanksgiving', which is an echo of the prayer *Memento* in the Latin mass, containing the words *hoc sacrificium laudis*, which refer to the whole eucharistic action. Further on, we find the words, 'and here we offer and present unto thee, O Lord, ourselves, our souls and bodies, to be a reasonable, holy and lively sacrifice unto thee.' It has sometimes been objected that this liturgy substitutes the offering or sacrifice of our own sinful selves for the one acceptable sacrifice of Christ, but I think this is a misconception. The idea of a self-offering of the worshippers did not originate with Cranmer or the Reformers, but goes back to the early centuries. The people, as the Body of Christ, are united with him in his sacrifice. So Augustine can say, 'The mystery of yourselves is laid upon the table of the Lord.'[10] Thus we offer ourselves to God only in and with Jesus Christ as united with his self-offering, and this finds expression in the words that the worshippers may be 'made one Body with thy Son Jesus Christ, that he may dwell in them and they in him'. This relation between Christ and his followers, sometimes called the 'double indwelling', has been the subject of controversy over its meaning for Cranmer. It appears again in the 1549 rite in the Prayer of Humble Access, which in turn was included in later editions of the Prayer Book. Perhaps again it has to be said that what exactly the words may have meant to Cranmer does not determine what they mean in the public liturgy of the Church of England. In any case, as Cyril Richardson points out, Cranmer was not clear and consistent in such matters. The words seem to have their ultimate origin in the Gospel of John, where the Father is in the Son and the Son in the Father, and this implies the most intimate personal union. But to return to the Prayer of Consecration. The language of sacrifice continues: 'And although we be unworthy to offer unto thee any sacrifice, yet we beseech thee to accept this our bounden duty and service.' This last phrase most naturally refers to the whole eucharistic action, offered to the Father as the only perfect oblation. The 1549 book added at this point a picturesque detail, taken from the Latin mass, in which it is asked that the angels may bring the people's 'prayers and supplications' into the divine presence. This detail was omitted in later versions of the Prayer Book.

However, the sacrificial language I have quoted remained for the most part unchanged in the most Protestant revision of the Prayer Book, that of 1552, and eventually passed into the book of 1662 which still remains the official liturgy of the Church of England. I do not think we have found it necessary to strain the interpretation in order to find in this main line of Anglican liturgical tradition a doctrine of eucharistic sacrifice which does not conflict with the insistence upon the uniqueness of the historical sacrifice on Calvary.

Indeed, the traditional Anglican Eucharist goes far towards combining the many aspects of the sacrament, and it is the mark of a good liturgy that it does bring to expression the different aspects of the Christian faith that are included within the Eucharist. Some liturgies suffer from one-sided emphases, and although in this chapter I am commending the sacrificial character of the Eucharist, I do not think it should be stressed to the point where it unduly overshadows other essential meanings of the sacrament. It is unfortunate that sometimes there is a tension between the understanding of the Eucharist as sacrifice and the Eucharist as communion or sacred meal. Even within living memory, many Roman Catholic and some Anglican churches had as the principal act of worship on Sundays a non-communicating High Mass at which only the clergy received the sacrament. This certainly exalted the sense of the sacrifice, but it did so only by mutilating the Eucharist as a whole by excising from it one of its integral moments, the communion of the people, the feeding of the faithful with the body and blood of Christ. Sometimes the communion rail was actually removed so that the congregation could have an uninterrupted view of the ceremonies, and this could hardly fail to make the worshippers feel that they were spectators rather than

participants in what was going on. It is true that there were
opportunities for the faithful to receive communion at low
masses earlier in the day, but only a few were sufficiently devout
to turn out twice on a Sunday morning, and the general result
was to discourage frequent communion. The liturgical problem
is to celebrate the Eucharist in such a way that its integrity is
not damaged, that the sacrifice will not be obscured by the
communion or the communion by the sacrifice. It seems to me
that the Anglican Eucharist was successful in holding these
things together, especially by including the self-offering of the
people under the concept of the sacrifice. They are made one
with Christ through receiving the communion of his body and
blood and so can be joined with him in his own acceptable
sacrifice.

Much of what I have been saying was clearly expressed in an
important but strangely neglected document from Anglican
history, the letter known as *Saepius officio*, which the Archbishops of Canterbury and York (at that time, Frederick
Temple and William Maclagan) addressed to 'the whole body
of bishops of the Catholic Church' in 1897, the year following
the condemnation of Anglican orders by Pope Leo XIII in the
bull *Apostolicae curae*.[11] It had been complained in the bull that
Anglican priests do not offer a sacrifice in the Eucharist and
therefore cannot be recognized as priests at all. In their reply,
the Archbishops claimed that the Church of England does
indeed have an adequate doctrine of eucharistic sacrifice. I
quote a paragraph which is, I think, the heart of their letter:

We make provision with the greatest reverence for the consecration of the Holy Eucharist, and commit it only to
properly ordained priests and to no other ministers of the
Church. Further, we truly teach the doctrine of eucharistic
sacrifice, and do not believe it to be 'a nude commemoration
of the sacrifice of the cross', an opinion which seems to be
attributed to us [by some Roman Catholic clerics]. But we
think it sufficient in the liturgy which we use in celebrating
the Holy Eucharist – while lifting up our hearts to the Lord,
and when now consecrating the gifts already offered that
they may become to us the body and blood of the Lord Jesus
Christ – to signify the sacrifice which is offered at that point

of the service in such terms as these. We continue a perpetual
memory of the precious death of Christ, who is our Advocate
with the Father and the Propitiation for our sins, according
to his precept, until his coming again. For first we offer the
sacrifice of praise and thanksgiving; then next we plead and
represent before the Father the sacrifice of the cross, and by
it we confidently entreat remission of sins and all other benefits of the Lord's passion for all the whole Church; and lastly
we offer the sacrifice of ourselves to the Creator of all things
which we have already signified by the oblations of his
creatures. This whole action, in which the people has necessarily to take its part, we are accustomed to call the Eucharistic Sacrifice.

If they had been writing today, the Archbishops could have
found in some of the revised liturgies of the twentieth century,
including the revised American Prayer Book and the English
Alternative Services Book, even stronger and more explicit
language about sacrifice than they found in the traditional
material. But it is important to note that they did vindicate the
essential catholicity of the Anglican position from the classic
documents of the Church of England, not even calling to witness the liturgies of the Scottish and American Episcopal
Churches, in which a 'prayer of oblation' had long formed part
of the canon. But what is perhaps most striking here is the closeness between what the Archbishops were saying in 1897 and
what Anglican and Roman Catholic scholars, appointed by
their several Churches, were saying in their 'agreed statement'
of 1971. Does any serious problem that was troubling con-
sciences in 1896 still remain?
    Perhaps one has to say that some obscurities and ambiguities
remain. But could it be otherwise? Newman and the other
'fathers' of the Oxford Movement prized what they called the
'principle of reserve'. This simply means that in theology there
is a danger that one may try to be too detailed, too explicit, too
analytic in probing matters of belief. This idea of reserve may
have been present in the minds of the two Archbishops whom
I have been quoting, for they also said, 'The matter [i.e.,
eucharistic sacrifice] is indeed one full of mystery and fitted to
draw onwards the minds of men by strong feelings of love and

piety to high and deep thoughts. But inasmuch as it ought to be treated with the highest reverence and to be considered a bond of Christian charity rather than an occasion for subtle disputations, too precise definitions of the nature of the sacrifice, or of the relation which unites the sacrifice of the eternal Priest and the sacrifice of the Church, which in some way certainly are one, ought in our opinion to be avoided rather than pressed into prominence.'

Perhaps indeed it is the language of poetry, liturgy, doxology, that grasps and expresses the mystery better than the language of scientific theology. There is a great Anglican eucharistic hymn which seems to me to say it all. It comes from the very peak of the Catholic revival, from the year 1874, and was written by William Bright, a Canon of Christ Church, Oxford:

> And now, O Father, mindful of the love
> That bought us once for all on Calvary's tree,
> And having with us him that pleads above,
> We here present, we here spread forth to thee,
> That only offering perfect in thine eyes,
> The one true pure immortal sacrifice.[12]

Benediction of the Blessed Sacrament

The Holy Eucharist is the centre of all Christian worship and spirituality, and there can be no substitute for it. It is described in the *Book of Common Prayer* as 'our bounden duty and service', for it is the way appointed by our Lord for the recalling of him. For the past hundred years and more, the Church has been engaged in stressing the centrality of the Eucharist, and has tried to ensure that its place is not usurped by other devotions, public or private, however laudable these may be. The duty and privilege of the Christian is to play his part in offering the eucharistic sacrifice and in receiving the Holy Communion.

We may be grateful that so much has been done to restore the Eucharist to its rightful place and to promote a better understanding of it. But the aim must be to extend the action and meaning of the Eucharist out from the centre to the furthest edges of life, so that the whole of life is conformed to the living Lord who gives himself to us at the altar. While it is right to stress the priority of the Eucharist, it would be a mistake if we were led to neglect or despise other acts of worship which have their proper place in the building up of the Christian life. The Eucharist, with the fullest participation of all the members of the body of Christ, is the indispensable centre, but there are many additional acts of devotion which help to extend it into all our activities and relationships and to increase our awareness of the sacramental character of creation. Such an act of devotion is Benediction of the Blessed Sacrament, and in this chapter I want to say something about its meaning and value.

I remember very well the first occasion on which I was present at Benediction. This happened many years ago at what was, for me, an important moment in life. I was serving in the British army and had received notice of posting overseas. I had been home for my last leave and was now waiting with other troops in a transit centre in the London area until we would be ordered to the ship that was to take us to Egypt. On the Sunday evening before we sailed, I was wandering through the streets of a sprawling suburban area near to where we were stationed. I came to an Anglican church, St Andrew's, Willesden Green, I think it was. The bell was summoning the people, and I went in. The first part of the service was familiar to me, for it was Evensong, with its splendid collects and canticles, its psalms and readings from Scripture. But then followed something new to me, though I had indeed read about it and was able to understand what was going on – the Benediction of the Blessed Sacrament. No doubt I was in an impressionable mood that night, but this service meant a great deal to me. Evensong had already meant much, but now, as it were, an additional dimension, the sacramental dimension, was also opened up. I did not know what lay ahead of me or when I might come back to these shores again, but I had been assured of our Lord's presence and had received his sacramental blessing. I was reminded of Jacob, when he was far from home at Bethel and heard the divine voice: 'Behold, I am with you and will keep you wherever you go, and will bring you back to this land; for I will not leave you until I have done that of which I have spoken to you.'[1] Yet I was not quite in the situation of Jacob, for whereas he had been altogether alone, I had been made aware of God's presence among his people, gathered to worship him.

Looking back, I do not think I am wrong in seeing in this incident a step on the way by which God, in his merciful providence, was calling me into the fulness of Christian faith and worship. In the years that followed, both overseas and after I returned home, whenever I had an opportunity to attend at the service of Benediction, I never failed to find in it the strength that comes from knowing that Christ is near. I learned also to perceive further depths of meaning in this impressive act of worship. To know that Christ is near is to experience both his grace and his judgment, and to be placed in our Lord's presence is to be searched by him as well as sustained by him.

There can be no doubt that in a very real way Benediction meets a legitimate need of many Christians. This need is one that has always been felt in religion, at least, by some types of people. It is the need to have before us some concrete manifestation of the divine reality, toward which we can direct our devotion. As Baron von Hügel was never tired of saying, spirit and sense go together in religion. It is true that the demand of sense for some visible, tangible manifestation of deity can lead to an idolatry if we let our minds rest in the visible manifestation, rather than letting it lead our thoughts into the unseen mystery of God; and this kind of idolatry happened often enough, both in the history of Israel and then in that of the Church. But one does not avoid the tendency to idolatry by turning away from sense. For there is just as great a danger, and possibly a more serious one, if we try to do without the objects of sense as if we were purely rational or purely spiritual beings; the danger in this case is that of pride and spiritual idolatry, and there are many instances of this in the history of puritan and iconoclastic sects.

Spirit and sense go together. This is obviously true in the Eucharist itself, where material elements are used as the vehicles of its inward spiritual action. As I have said already, it is above all in the eucharistic action that Christ comes to his people and they know his presence, so that this is the central act of worship. But Christ's promise is to be with us *always*.[2] So at a very early period in the Church's history, there arose the practice of reservation of the Blessed Sacrament. At first this was for the sick, but soon the practice took on a wider significance. In those days because of the ever threatening dangers of persecution celebrations of the Eucharist could not be frequent, and between celebrations the faithful reserved the Sacrament in their homes (or even carried it about on their persons) and from time to time they communicated themselves from it. It must have kept them always mindful that Christ was with them in his living presence, and thus it is not surprising that when the times of persecution had passed, the Sacrament continued to be reserved, but now in churches where people might go to pray and worship in the very presence of Christ.

A further step was taken in the Middle Ages. In the great surge of eucharistic devotion which arose at that time, there

grew up the practice of exposition of the Blessed Sacrament. The
sense of living presence, already ensured by the reservation of
the Sacrament, was intensified by opening the doors of the
tabernacle or even by exhibiting the Host on a throne in a
monstrance. This practice is easily understandable for, as St
Augustine noted, seeing has a priority among the senses.[3] Everyone has a strong desire to see that which excites his interest or
claims his attention. There is a directness in seeing, a sense of the
immediate presence of what is seen. The end of the Christian
life is the *vision* of God. We feel that a person is really present to
us when we are able to look upon him, face to face. It is simply
a fact of human psychology that the worshippers' awareness of
the Lord's presence was intensified and brought home in a lively
way as they looked with their eyes upon the spotless Host.

At some time too along the way there developed another
practice, still to be observed in many churches. The priest, in
delivering the Communion, would first make the sign of the
cross with the Host over the head of the recipient. This is perhaps an unnecessary elaboration in the midst of the Eucharist
itself, but the meaning and intention are entirely admirable, and
one can see how there is the possibility of employing this sacramental blessing outside of the immediate context of giving
communion.

It was from a combination of the practices described that the
service of Benediction came into being. The practices were
wedded to some magnificent wording, drawn partly from the
Psalter, partly from the eucharistic hymns and prayers of St
Thomas Aquinas, and partly from the devotions of a late
eighteenth-century Jesuit priest, Louis Felici. Thus, in response
to the needs of the worshipping community, there finally crystal-
lized the service of Benediction as we know it today. In its
finished form, it is a relatively modern act of devotion, but part
of its appeal is just that it has gathered up in itself elements from
the whole history of the worship of the people of God – the
virility of the Old Testament, the steadfast faith of the early
Church, the glowing piety of the Middle Ages, the continuing
devotion of the Church as the cold winds of the Enlightenment
and the modern age begin to blow upon it.

I am well aware that critics of Benediction would brush aside
as unimportant many of the things that I have so far said about

the value of this act of worship. They would say – and they would be right about this – that one cannot justify an act of worship on the grounds of personal preference or what it has meant in one's own personal history, and that one cannot even justify it in terms of its meeting general psychological needs, and still less on the grounds of aesthetic excellence. Benediction might qualify on all of these counts, but in the long run the only convincing justification must be to show that this particular act of devotion has a sound theological basis. But it seems to me that it will not be difficult to expound such a basis, especially when we remember that so much of the wording of Benediction is taken straight from St Thomas, himself a very prince of theologians.

If there is one theme that runs clearly through St Thomas' writings, it is surely this, that when we look on creaturely beings within the world and consider them 'in depth', so to speak, our mind is carried beyond them to that divine Being by whom every creature exists and whom every creature in greater or less degree makes manifest. This theme is plainly stated in the foundations of St Thomas' theology, when he discourses on the 'five ways' by which the mind rises from the consideration of the created world to the apprehension of God, on whom the world depends. But it is essentially the same theme that gets expressed in his magnificent eucharistic hymns, which speak of the 'glory' hidden 'beneath these shadows mean' and of how 'faith, our outward sense befriending, makes the inward vision clear'.

The theme is precisely what one might expect to find in a Christian theologian, for Christianity is the religion of the incarnation. It proclaims that 'the Word became flesh and dwelt among us, full of grace and truth.'[4] Thus Archbishop William Temple could say that Christianity 'is the most avowedly materialist of all the great religions.'[5] It is so because through its faith in the incarnation it sets a new value on the material world and understands it as a vehicle for divine grace and truth. This is a sacramental world where creaturely being becomes transparent so that we can see through to the God from whom all things flow. There is an intimate connection linking natural theology, the incarnation, the Eucharist and the sacramental principle generally. In every case, we are led beyond the immediate objects of sense to the creative reality of God.

God does not leave us with just some vague general knowledge of himself, to be culled from the creation at large. It is true that St Thomas believed that there is a 'natural theology' and that every thinking man can form some idea of God and arrive at an assurance of his reality. But beyond this, St Thomas and all Christians have believed also in God's revelation, by which he has himself enlarged and purified our knowledge of him. We may think of 'revelation' as meaning that at particular times and places and in particular events and persons, but always in and through worldly realities, God has communicated himself, focussing, as it were, his presence and causing to shine brightly and clearly before men that knowledge of himself which otherwise they can only dimly grasp. A revelation is a glimpse of the glory that is always there but may be in greater or less degree hidden. The great events in Israel's history were revelations of this kind. Above all, Jesus Christ was 'the true light that lightens every man'.[6] He was and remains the great focus of God's presence and acting in the world.

But Christ in turn appointed the bread and wine of the Eucharist to be the focus in which generations to come would find anew his presence. Whether we speak of transubstantiation or consubstantiation, of transignification or transfinalization, or whether we are content – as the Church was for many centuries – simply to acknowledge the mystery of eucharistic presence without trying to spell it out too precisely in philosophical categories, the classic liturgies of the Church have consistently affirmed the real presence of the Church's Lord in the material elements consecrated in the Eucharist. They become for Christians the focus of a wider presence. It is in terms of this focussing of our Lord's presence that the service of Benediction is to be understood – and also justified, if anyone thinks that it needs justifying. Psychologically speaking, we need some concrete visible manifestation toward which to direct our devotion; while theologically speaking, this is already provided for us by our Lord's gracious manifestation of his presence in the Blessed Sacrament.

When this is understood, complaints about 'idolatry' and 'fetichism' (which one sometimes hears) are seen to be beside the point and theologically misinformed. Let us assure any who may be perturbed over such matters that we are not being so stupid as to worship a wafer, nor do we have such an archaic

and myth-laden mentality as to suppose that the object before us
is charged with some magical power. Rather, it is in and through
the Sacrament that we adore Christ, and through him the triune
God. We do it in this manner because, we being men and not
angels, have need of an earthly manifestation of the divine
presence; and because he, in his grace and mercy, has promised
to grant us his presence in this particular manifestation and in
this particular meeting place.

With these thoughts in mind, let us now turn to consider in
somewhat more detail what takes place at Benediction. It is an
amazingly simple and beautifully proportioned act of worship,
and although it is very brief, it has a wonderful completeness.
We can think of it as made up of three main parts.

The key word for describing the first part is 'contemplation'.
The doors of the tabernacle are opened, the Host is exposed in a
monstrance and censed, and two great hymns of St Thomas are
sung, *O salutaris* and *Tantum ergo*, honouring the 'saving Victim'
who in his love comes to be with his people in 'this great Sacrament'. Sometimes there is a period of silence between the
hymns, or a motet is sung. I want to stress the word 'contemplation'. We desperately need more of this, for even in our religion
nowadays we are most of the time so busy talking or doing things
or going places that Christ hardly gets a chance to say anything
to us. While the modern liturgical movement has rightly tried
to wean people away from the notion that they are just spectators or auditors at worship, it has, I believe, stressed too much
what *we do*, and too little what *comes to us from God*. It is good for
us just to let God soak into us, so to speak, and surely this does
happen as we direct our gaze to the saving Victim and kneel
quietly in his presence. As the hymn ends, we hear the words:
'Thou gavest them bread from heaven.'[7] We are reminded of
how God fed his people with manna in the wilderness, how his
providence never forsakes us, and, above all, how he has come
to us in Jesus Christ who called himself 'the living bread which
came down from heaven'.[8] This first part of the act of worship is
then summed up in the beautiful collect which St Thomas com-
posed for the Feast of Corpus Christi, and in which we pray that
we may so 'venerate the sacred mysteries of thy body and blood
that we may ever perceive within ourselves the fruit of thy
redemption'.

There follows immediately the second main part of the service, and this is also its climax – the actual sacramental blessing of the people. The priest, taking up the monstrance, turns and makes with the Host the sign of the cross over the people. Following on the quiet mood of contemplation, this change to movement and action has a significance which is, I believe, well illustrated from some impressive words of Hugh Blenkin: 'God can never be the object of man's worship, he is always the subject.'[9] This is the meaning of the blessing that is given in the midst of this act of devotion. God is always ahead of us, and our worship is response. He takes the initiative and comes to us, before we think of turning to him. Now at the very heart of our time of devotion he gives us his blessing through Christ. I have related above how this blessing once came to me unsought and unexpected, and I hope that it will always mean as much to me and to others.

The third part of the service is our spontaneous response of praise and thanksgiving. 'Blessed be God!' we say, using the words of the Divine Praises, attributed to the Jesuit Felici. These Divine Praises bless God for the many ways in which he has been present and has manifested himself in the world – in the name by which he made himself known, in Christ the incarnate Word, in the Sacrament, in the Holy Spirit, in the Blessed Virgin, in all the saints. How indeed could we have known him at all, if he had not manifested himself in earthly and historical realities? Then, as the final burst of praise, comes the psalm *Laudate Dominum*,[10] calling on all nations to praise the Lord for his merciful kindness and truth and pointing to that consummation when the whole creation will adore. It makes a fitting end to a great act of adoration of God in Christ.

Benediction is very much an act of waiting on God, of letting him make his presence known, of letting him speak to us. We are told that 'they who wait for the Lord shall renew their strength'.[11] Certainly, this act of devotion offers an important opportunity to renew our strength, and one wishes that its value were more widely appreciated in the Church. The best place for Benediction is probably after evensong or vespers. We hear much nowadays about the desirability of holding Word and Sacrament together, and though this is usually taken to mean that the ministry of the Word should receive greater emphasis at the Eucharist, it equally implies that at services centred on the Word, such as evensong or vespers, it is desirable to add the sacramental dimension, supplied by Benediction. Certainly, it is an enrichment of Christian worship and makes a valuable contribution toward building up the disciple in the Christian faith and life. 'Let us for ever adore Christ in the most holy Sacrament!'

XI

The Daily Offices

To spend a few days in retreat living with a religious community in a monastery or convent is like moving into a different kind of world. There are all sorts of differences, but perhaps the fundamental one is that time is ordered by the hours of prayer – 'the hours in order flow'. In the secular world, we are very much aware of the passage of time, and in varying degrees we are all subject to the clock. We are subject also to regular patterns of behaviour which may be dull and routine. But when one's life is caught up in a time ordered by prayer, this is quite different from the pressures and routines of our everyday experience of time. One is no longer trying to get the most out of the time at one's disposal in the way of production or consumption, trying to beat the clock, as we say. And one does not feel that a pattern of action has been imposed, but that one is participating in a creative rhythm which, though ordered, is liberating. Not least, it is liberating from the anxiety that one will not have time for . . .

The liturgical ordering of time is a complex matter and several components enter into it. Here I am concerned with the daily hours of prayer known as the divine office. 'Seven times a day I praise thee for thy righteous ordinances,'[1] wrote a psalmist. The habit of having regular hours of prayer each day established itself among the Jews and eventually passed into the Christian Church. Traditionally, there was a night office, which came to be called mattins, and the seven daylight offices called lauds, prime, terce, sext, none, vespers and compline. This arrangement persisted for many centuries in the Church, though in fact some of the offices came to be said together in groups and more recently there have been moves toward the reduction and simplification of the scheme. But the actual number of offices is unimportant – clearly this is one of those matters which will vary from one group of people to another.[2] About this I shall say something more later. What is important about the offices is not their frequency but simply that they provide the basis for a prayerful ordering of time.

Several times I have used the words 'order' and 'ordering'. We must look more closely at what these words mean. Near the beginning of this book, H. H. Price was quoted as saying that the religious man appears to be 'more at home' in the universe and that as a consequence he has a certain serenity and peace.[3] I think that both the feeling of 'being at home' and the quality of serenity are closely connected with the question of order. Let us think again of the man or woman from secular life going for a time on retreat with a religious community. Such a person's life is caught up in an order, and an order implies reliability. He finds himself in a serene community, in an atmosphere of stability and trustworthiness where it is possible to be at home. For one can only be at home if there is some dependable order. This holds at the level of the physical world. It has been possible to develop a scientific understanding of nature because there is an order in the world and things do not just happen at random. Not only science but daily life is made possible on the basis of such an order. This means that in a genuine sense we trust nature. Human society has developed an order of a different kind. This too is necessary for daily life. Sometimes the social and political order is invoked to suppress freedom, but on the other hand there could be no freedom without a basis of law to make it possible and to protect it.

Religious faith, however, implies a trust in an order beyond either the order of physical nature or the order of human society. This is divine order, an order of love and justice which embraces and underlies all order. The prayerful ordering of time is a way by which men keep themselves in constant aware- ness of the divine order – an awareness which is both supportive, because it carries the feeling of being at home in a dependable universe, and demanding, because it sets before us a transcen- dent moral standard.

The idea of a correspondence between the rhythm of prayer and worship on the one side and a cosmic order or rhythm on the other is, of course, common in the history of religion. For instance, the ancient Indian concept of *rta* (cognate with English 'rite') visualized an order both ethical and metaphysical which found expression in and was in turn maintained by the practice of religion. The cosmic significance of prayer has been recognized in various ways in the Christian tradition. The prayer of the Church has been understood as part of the response of all creation to God and as joined 'in a wonderful order' with the adoration of angels, who may be taken as representative of the whole range of rational and spiritual beings who have existed or do exist or will exist in this universe in addition to the race of men. 'The real significance of the divine office,' wrote Evelyn Underhill, 'is that in its recitation the individual or group enters the ancient cycle of prayer, by which day by day and hour by hour the Church in the name of all creation adores and implores the eternal God.'[4]

So far we have been thinking of the offices chiefly in the traditional extended form which was developed in monastic communities. There will always, we hope, be some men and women whose main work will be explicitly prayer, and we must remember that just as the Church prays not for itself alone but 'in the name of all creation', so those members of the Church who have wholly given themselves to the life of prayer are praying not for themselves alone but in the name of the whole Church. But those in the religious orders will always be a small minority, and my concern is to commend the office in some form to those whose lives are spent in avocations in the world. Is it possible for them – the doctor, the parish priest, the factory worker, the shop assistant, the teacher and the rest – to know in the disordered world of human affairs anything of that serenity which perhaps they glimpsed in a few precious hours spent on retreat? When one has duties to perform, trains to catch, deadlines to observe and so on, how can there be anything like a prayerful ordering of time? It is unreasonable to expect even the busy parish priest to observe the full quota of traditional hours. There is in fact a curious paradox to be noted. To join a religious community is, in one sense, to surrender all worldly security, to abandon everything for the sake of God. And yet, as members of these communities tell us, to divest oneself of worldly goods is also to be set free from cares and to have the security of an ordered existence which the world cannot touch. The religious life is not any more difficult than life in a secular career, and not any more meritorious. Each mode of life brings its own problems and testings.

The problem for the person living under the strains and stresses of the everyday world is how to combine order and freedom. How can one have a rule of prayer that will be flexible enough to allow one to meet the incessant and unpredictable demands made upon one's time, and yet firm enough to provide a basis of order that preserves some serenity (or even sanity) and prevents life from degenerating into a meaningless succession of more or less unrelated tasks and enjoyments? How can there be a prayerful ordering of time outside of the monastery walls when one must also be free for the innumerable demands of family, work, neighbour, civic responsibility and all the rest? This is the question which Bonhoeffer faced, using a musical metaphor which is not very far removed from our foregoing discussion about the ordering of life. Bonhoeffer talked about the 'polyphony' of life. 'What I mean is that God wants us to love him eternally with our whole hearts – not in such a way as to injure or weaken our earthly love, but to provide a kind of *cantus firmus* to which the other melodies of life provide the counterpoint.'[5] The *cantus firmus* is the recurring rhythmic pattern which serves as the basis for the music, giving it a unity and consistency. Translated into spiritual terms, it is the recurring cycle of prayer and communing with God which gives, as it were, the dominant 'set' to life. But over that *cantus firmus* all kinds of distinct melodies may be heard interweaving in a complex texture.

Incidentally, it is odd that Bonhoeffer has been sometimes held up as an exemplar of religionless Christianity. To be sure, he certainly believed that the Christian must be involved in the secular world, and he himself became implicated in the political arena in a major way. But if religion is understood in terms of prayer, then to the end of his days Bonhoeffer seems to have been a very religious man.[6] Both in the seminary which he ran and later in prison, he was moving toward the monastic ideal. The kind of religion he criticized was not the regular offices, central to life and providing a *cantus firmus* giving meaning and order, but religion brought in as something marginal and therefore dispensable, a few prayers here and there when one happens to be in the mood.

But, to return to our main theme, the *cantus firmus*, I should think, must take different forms for different people. For most, the traditional offices are too numerous, too time-consuming and too cumbrous. For some, perhaps one brief office in the day will suffice, or be all that there is time for. It has also been suggested that a revised and enriched lectionary for the Eucharist[7] might eventually take the place of the office which would be superseded as a separate exercise. However, I think that there are still many people (and I would count myself among them) who believe that a classic solution to the problem of the offices continues to be viable for our time – I mean, of course, Cranmer's work of genius in condensing the traditional scheme of hours into the two Prayer Book offices of mattins and evensong. No doubt his work is susceptible of improvements in points of detail,[8] but I have deliberately called it a work of genius, for in their essentials mattins and evensong remain unrivalled as daily offices for those whose vocations lie in the world. They are sufficiently brief (fifteen to twenty minutes each) so that most people who are really in earnest about the matter will find time for them. Yet they are sufficiently solid to provide a genuine *cantus firmus*, an immersion into the meaning of Christian faith adequate to the point where it can really shape life.

The morning and evening offices of the Prayer Book are built chiefly out of the psalms, the scriptures and the prayers of the Church, so that the order embodied in these offices itself brings together three distinct cycles. Let us briefly consider them in turn, and inquire about their value.

In Cranmer's scheme, the whole of the Psalter is read in course each month. Two questions call for an answer: are the psalms still important enough to have such a large place in the Church's worship, and even if they are, is it desirable to use the whole of the Psalter?

I think the first of these questions must be answered in the affirmative. There is no comparable body of religious poetry setting forth God's saving work and man's response (or lack of response). Admittedly, the psalms come from pre-Christian times. But although they originated in Old Testament religion, they have been used continuously by the people of God, Jewish and Christian, and something of their depth is revealed by the fact that in the long history of their use they have taken on fresh meanings and perhaps they will take on new meanings in the future. Christians have found in the psalms anticipations of many things in their own faith – the passion of Christ, the Eucharist, the Church and so on – and although these ideas were not present to the minds of the original Hebrew poets, nevertheless they become legitimate interpretations as the history of God's dealings unfolds itself. 'If we Christians wish to understand the psalms', writes Drijvers, 'we must bear in mind that the roots of their thought lie in the past, in the Old Testament, while their blossoming reaches out into the far future, to the end of the world, to heaven itself.'[9] The psalms are living entities, still capable of yielding meaning and of stimulating spiritual growth; and when one remembers how much the psalms have been involved in Christian theology and spirituality over the centuries, it will not seem too much to read them through once a month.

But is it desirable to read the Psalter straight through, as it is set out in the Prayer Book? The psalms are not all of equal value, and there are a few which it has become something of an embarrassment to read in public. Complaints are directed most often against those psalms which call on God to take vengeance on his enemies. We have to be careful, however, not to become sentimental on this matter. Though we would not identify ourselves with some of the utterances of the psalmists, we must recognize that there is a place in religion (if it has not gone soft) for righteous anger against oppression and the misuses of God's gifts. The psalmists no doubt oversimplified: 'Do not I hate them that hate thee, O Lord?'[10] But self-righteousness abounds as much in the Church today as it did among them, though now it is more subtle. To do the psalmists justice when they fulminate against the wicked, Roland Murphy tells us that 'one must appreciate the Old Testament desire to see God's justice manifested in the world (the only world of which the Israelite knew). There is no need to judge the personal experience and moral evaluation of the psalmist; he simply recognizes the evil man as opposed to God and hence as worthy of punishment.'[11] But even so, it seems to me desirable that there should be some gesture whereby the Christian use of the psalms shows that there is a better way than punishment. The omission of Psalm 58 from the morning series and Psalm 109 from the evening series is such a gesture, and there is much to be said for omitting or including psalms in their entirety, rather than snipping out verses here and there, for this can hardly fail to become a matter of personal likes and dislikes.

But in any case, it is not only the imprecatory passages that cause trouble. For my own part, I am more upset by the smug self-righteousness of Psalm 101 (and no commentator has been able to dispel this interpretation from my mind) than I am by the honest anger against the enemies of the Lord expressed in Psalm 83. I am equally embarrassed by having to read the utter nonsense of Psalm 110, the Hebrew text of which seems to be so corrupt that even the most ingenious translators will not be able to make sense of it. Yet to express these opinions shows how easy it is to become individualistic, and probably in the long run it is best simply to take the psalms as they come, recognizing that they have to be understood in the context of a long history. Even in some of the worst psalms one comes across a verse that is in itself a gem or that has received a Christian interpretation. But whether one makes cuts or takes the Psalter as a whole, it remains foundational for the daily office.

As regards the Holy Scriptures, Cranmer's wish was that they should be read in course, as far as possible, without too many interruptions by proper lessons. He devised a scheme whereby the Old Testament was read through once each year and the New Testament three times. Cranmer's original scheme has long since been superseded as it had a number of defects, but his general principles were good, particularly that the offices should provide for reading the Bible connectedly. His aim of covering the Old Testament and Apocrypha once a year and the New Testament three times was probably too concentrated a diet, and modern lectionaries have reduced it. Obviously the whole development of biblical studies since Cranmer's time has to be taken into account in drawing up a lectionary.

But I am not intending to discuss the problems of the lectionary. All I wish to do is to say that the systematic reading of the

Bible, as provided for in the daily offices, is an essential part of Christian spirituality. In much of this book I have stressed the sacramental aspects of spirituality, but it has certainly not been my intention to underrate the importance of the Bible. I affirm again that in a truly Christian spirituality Word and Sacrament must be held together. Knowledge of the Holy Scriptures is all important for the formation of intelligent Christian disciples. The regular reading of the Bible lays the foundation of such knowledge, but if there is to be genuine understanding of the Bible, then the reading must be supplemented by the use of commentaries and other helps. This shows the wisdom of the modern lectionaries in spreading the biblical material over a longer period, for this makes it more likely that it will be not only read but inwardly digested.

The third cycle which enters into the office is that of the Christian year. The cycle of seasons and feasts recalls to mind the history of God's acts and at the same time can be understood as stages on the way of the individual disciple. In this way also the office incorporates the individual into an order and a movement transcending his own little boundaries.

The daily offices are, on the one hand, a discipline, an order, a structure; but I have tried to show that they are also liberating and creative. At the present time, there is rebellion against order and structure, and the offices have not escaped this rebellion. Is there anything we learn from the psalms that we cannot learn better from life, from meeting our fellows? Cannot we hear the word of God from today's newspaper or the newest novel as well as from the Bible? I do not for a moment deny that immersion in life and in the culture of our time are of first importance, for Christian discipleship certainly does not happen in a vacuum. But we need immersion too in Christian truth if we are rightly to interpret life and culture, and that is the kind of immersion which those brief offices of mattins and evensong provide. The resources which they open up to us are so vast as to be inexhaustible, and I do not think that we could ever outgrow the offices. To reject their discipline is more likely to be a mark of pride than of maturity. One of the great spiritual masters of modern times, Baron von Hügel, mentions that at his own stage of maturity, his counsellor told him that his prayer should now be mainly informal but advised, among other things, one decade of the rosary every day 'this especially to help prevent (von Hügel's) interior life from losing touch with the devotion of the people.'[12] It could be argued with even greater force that the offices keep us in touch with the whole Church. They do not impede the individual's spiritual growth, but both nourish it and supply a standard by which it is to be judged.

Stations of the Cross

One of the most popular words in contemporary theology is 'participation'. The word is used in many ways. In the most general sense, to be a Christian is understood as participating in the mysteries of the life of Christ. In liturgical renewal, the aim is to promote the fullest participation of all present. In calls to social action, the Christian is urged to participate in the life of the world. If Christian faith is a commitment and not merely an intellectual belief, then the Christian cannot remain simply a hearer or a spectator – he must also be among the 'doers of the word'.[1] The great sacraments of the Church bring the idea of participation very clearly before us. To be dipped in the waters of baptism is to share in the dying and rising of Christ. To offer the Eucharist is to be joined with Christ in his sacrifice and to receive his life. Among other devotions, the one that perhaps most vividly encourages and fosters our active sharing in the life and ministry of our Lord is the one known as Stations of the Cross, or Way of the Cross. In this devotion, we walk with him along the way to Calvary.

In the earliest days, the Christian faith was known as 'the Way'. It was a way of life, and that way was modelled on the way that Christ himself had travelled, accompanied by the first disciples. It was the way that led up to Jerusalem and to the cross. According to John Baillie, 'when the next generation of Christians spoke of "the way", they meant that they were recapitulating the way he had travelled, his journey up to Jerusalem and to the crucifixion.'[2] They remembered the words of the Lord: 'If any man would come after me, let him deny himself and take up his cross and follow me.'[3]

The city of Jerusalem was destroyed by the Romans in AD 70, and the small Christian community had already fled to the countryside. But the memory of 'the way' remained, and when, in later and more stable times, Christian pilgrims began to visit Jersualem, they sought out the places associated with Jesus, and they began the practice of walking along the way from Pilate's house to Calvary, the *Via dolorosa* by which Christ had gone to his crucifixion.

Faith is not just a matter of the intellect. It involves the imagination and the emotions and, indeed, the whole life of man. We can readily understand that as these pilgrims went along the way, they felt themselves very close to Christ and the meaning of his life and atoning death was brought home to them in a new and lively manner. They understood more deeply too the meaning of the Christian life, with its demand that the disciple must learn the obedience of self-giving and self-sacrifice if he is to attain to fulness of life in Christ. For the disciple, the way of the cross still winds on in his own world.

To some, it may seem irrational that just to visit a place and to let its associations kindle the imagination and stir the feelings would deepen the commitment of faith. But so it happens with many people, and perhaps the man who is so coldly intellectual or so intensely practical that he can know nothing of this poetry of faith is a man to be pitied. 'To abstract the mind from all local emotion would be impossible if it were endeavoured, and would be foolish if it were possible. That man is little to be envied whose patriotism would not gain force upon the plain of Marathon, or whose piety would not grow warmer among the ruins of Iona!' So wrote Dr Samuel Johnson of the feelings he experienced when in the course of his tour to the Western Isles of Scotland he visited the scene of St Columba's labours.

Yet this is not just a matter of how we feel about things. Some students of history have insisted that to understand history is not merely to know what happened on some occasion or other or even the causes that brought it about, but to have an imaginative insight into the minds of the persons concerned on that occasion, so that we may be said almost to relive their experience. In the words of Ernst Troeltsch, the good historian's aim is 'to make an event as intelligible as if it were part of our own experience'.[4] Faith in the cross of Christ is more than either the belief that this event happened long ago or a doctrine of atoning sacrifice; it must also be a sharing in the event of the cross in such a way that its inner meaning and power are experienced by us now.

My own journey along that ancient and narrow way remains vividly in my memory though it is more than twenty-five years ago since I found myself in Jerusalem in the course of military service and made the pilgrimage with a group of soldiers. Our starting-point was the ancient stone pavement, excavated in recent years, where Pilate pronounced judgment.[5] From there we turned on to the *Via dolorosa*, stopping at each of the sites which either memory or pious imagination has associated with some event in our Lord's last journey. The pilgrimage ends in the Church of the Holy Sepulchre, reputedly built over the scene of Calvary and of the adjacent tomb in the garden.

Even in our own time, when travel is fast and easy, one does not expect to be visiting the Holy Land very often; and, of course, in earlier times a pilgrimage was so expensive and dangerous an undertaking that it was a once-in-a-lifetime experience, confined to a very few people indeed. Thus it is not surprising that medieval pilgrims hit upon the idea of having in their home parishes a form of devotion that would promote the same sense of participation in Christ's passion that they had known as they followed along the *Via dolorosa* in Jerusalem. Such a devotion would not only renew their own experience but would help to extend it to the far larger number of their fellow parishioners who would never visit the Holy Land at all. It was from these beginnings that the devotion developed until it assumed the form which we know today, with the fourteen stations represented by pictures or sculptures arranged round the church, so that the faithful might proceed from one to another and, through prayer and meditation before each, recall and participate in the events of our Lord's journey to the cross.

Let us now try to analyse this participation in more detail. If we are not just spectators gazing curiously at a series of pictures but are allowing these scenes to catch us up, as it were, so that we belong in them and it is as if, in Troeltsch's words, they 'were part of our own experience', then we must find ourselves identified with some or other of the personages in these scenes. However, we are such many-sided creatures that perhaps we do not quite know where we belong. Furthermore, we tend to identify ourselves in such ways as will show us in the best possible light, rather than in ways that may disconcert us by showing us too plainly who and what we really are.

As Christians, we live in the paradox that we are at once sinners and yet sinners who are justified in Christ. But this formula does not quite express our situation. It hardly makes clear that the Christian life is a movement, a progress, a discipline in which sin is being constantly overcome through grace. That is to say that the Christian life is a way of pilgrimage, summed up in the way of the cross, and it is because the devotion of the Stations of the Cross concentrates this way for us and so helps to shape the whole way of life that we follow, that this devotion can be a useful discipline, conforming our lives to Christ. This also means that as we follow out the devotion, we find ourselves at various levels of identification, just as there are various stages in the Christian life. In our life on earth, we do not pass once for all from one stage to another, and so in the Stations of the Cross we do not altogether leave one level of identification for another. But through their interaction, we are brought into a better understanding of ourselves in our relation to Christ, and in this devotion as in the Christian life, we are summoned from each level to the one above it and offered the grace whereby each step can be taken.

I think we can distinguish three levels on which we can identify as we go round the Stations and seek to let ourselves be caught up as participants in the scenes that they bring to mind. These three levels correspond approximately with the three stages which in classic spirituality have been traditionally distinguished on the Christian way – the purgative, a turning from sin and overcoming of evil; the illuminative, a growth in understanding and commitment; and the unitive, the goal of perfect union with God in Christ.

We begin in penitence with the acknowledgement that we and all men have 'sinned and come short of the glory of God'.[6] As we stand before the first station, which depicts Christ being condemned to death, we can identify ourselves only with the traducers, accusers, rejectors, condemners. 'My weak self-love and guilty pride his Pilate and his Judas were.' It is natural that the devotion of the Stations is specially associated with the penitential seasons of Lent and Passiontide, and yet the call to repentance is always relevant. Even if one may agree that traditional liturgies overstressed the penitential aspect,[7] this must not blind us to the fact that repentance must be the first step in any approach to God or any renewal of human life, and to acknowledge sin is already to have begun to turn away from it. And what can convict us of sin like this scene of Christ, condemned and rejected – not only by the men of his time but by ourselves and our fellows today, as we reject him again and again, in our personal lives, in our social institutions, in our international relations, and even in our lukewarm churches? Yet this very scene of Christ condemned is not merely convicting us of sin. If it were, we could only despair. It is also pointing us to the ineffable mystery of grace in the world, to the power of God at work in human history. This is the power that transforms our human situations and brings good out of evil. The Christ condemned is he whom God has 'appointed heir of all things'.[8] The Christ who convicts us of sin is the Christ who invites us to let the mystery of his grace work in us.

But we must not try to hurry on too quickly from that first mood of penitence or look for a more desirable role with which to identify in these scenes of the passion, before we have fully acknowledged our solidarity with the disfiguring evil of the world. At the other stations too we must acknowledge this. The more truly we acknowledge it, the deeper will be our longing for an openness to the grace of renewal.

As we respond to this grace, we are summoned to a new level of identification. We are summoned to be disciples, and so to a discipline. A disciple is a learner and his discipline is the training whereby he learns. To learn the way of the cross is the hardest thing of all, and the training by which we are to advance in this learning is provided for us by the discipline of prayer and worship. Those who disparage prayer and worship and imagine that without these one can achieve some kind of instant Christianity do not know what they are talking about. They understand neither the weakness of our humanity nor the depth and richness of the spiritual maturity into which Christ is calling us.

Those who have advanced far along the road of discipleship toward maturity and proficiency are the saints. We meet several of them in the course of the Stations, and in seeking to identify ourselves as disciples we may fasten our aspirations on them. At the fifth station we recall how St Simon of Cyrene helped to carry the cross.[9] We are told that he was 'compelled' to do this, but even if he first rendered service to Christ involuntarily, the tradition records that he went on to become a faithful disciple. He was not broken but liberated and made a new man by the burden that was laid on him. At the next station, we are reminded of the story of St Veronica who refreshed Christ as he passed by wiping his face with a cloth and found his features imprinted on it. Though a legend, the story is none the less a true parable of how Christ grants his own likeness to those who offer their service in sincerity and devotion. Near the end of the Stations, we meet St Joseph of Arimathea who obtained the body of Christ from Pilate and laid it in the tomb. Joseph is described as 'a respected member of the council'.[10] It must have needed a lot of courage for this 'establishment' figure to come out into the open and reveal his sympathy for Jesus and his outcast band. If we truly learn Christ from the saints and participate in their commitments, then we shall be learning to help carry the neighbour's cross in today's world and to render the costly service that is demanded of the Christian.

The highest reach of sainthood we ascribe to the Blessed Virgin, and at the third station we recall her meeting with her Son on that fateful journey of his. Yet she is also our companion along the entire way, for the hymn that is sung as the procession moves from station to station is the *Stabat Mater*. Who was closer to him in his passion than his mother? Mary is the type of the Church, its purest manifestation. Through her the Lord became incarnate in the world, and she identified with him in his self-giving love with a poignancy and intensity that we can scarcely imagine. She still sets the standard for the Church of today and the disciple of today, for it is through the Church that Christ must now become incarnate and visible in the world, and this happens in turn through the disciple's willingness to share in his sacrifice.

So we are pointed to the final level of identification – union with Christ himself in the fulfilling of his reconciling ministry and in his oneness with the Father, the source of all grace for life and creativity and love. To be conformed to Christ is the goal of Christian prayer and devotion and the aim of spiritual

discipline. Already we live 'in Christ' and we acknowledge that
both baptism and the Eucharist imply our participation in his
dying and rising. In the strength of Christ, we are called to
'complete what is lacking in Christ's afflictions for the sake of his
body'.[11] 'The way of the Cross', writes Michael Quoist, 'winds
through our towns and cities, our hospitals and factories, and
through our battlefields . . . It is in front of these new Stations
of the Cross that we must stop and meditate and pray to the
suffering Christ for strength to love him enough and to act.'[12]

Some Christian disciples have written of identification with
Christ in language of great boldness. For instance, in reply to
the objection of Celsus that God had sent only one Christ into
a corner of the world when he might have incarnated the divine
Spirit in many bodies all over the world, Origen declares: 'If
anyone should want to see many bodies filled with a divine
Spirit, ministering to the salvation of men everywhere after the
pattern of the one Christ, let him realize that those who in many
places teach the doctrine of Jesus rightly and live an upright
life are themselves also called Christs by the divine scriptures in
the words: "Touch not my Christs and do my prophets no
harm" . . . Knowing that Christ has come, we see that because
of him there have been many Christs in the world who, like him,
have "loved righteousness and hated iniquity".'[13] We find
similar language in Luther: 'Just as our neighbour is in need and
lacks that in which we abound, so we also have been in need
before God and have lacked his mercy. Hence, as our heavenly
Father has in Christ freely come to our help, we also ought
freely to help our neighbour through our body and its works,
and each should become as it were a Christ to the other, that we
may be Christs to one another and Christ may be the same in all;
that is, that we may be truly Christians.'[14]

To be sure, such language as I have quoted can be dangerous
if it obliterates the uniqueness of Jesus Christ or obscures the
disciple's dependence upon him. Yet it is also a language which
takes discipleship with utter seriousness. Full identification with
Christ is an eschatological goal, yet it is one that may really be
hoped for. But the ultimate consummation of this union we
glimpse only fitfully and dimly. For most of the time we waver
uncertainly between penitence and the lower levels of discipleship. Yet our faith and hope is that the mystery of grace, made

manifest in Christ, works in us and in the whole Church, and indeed in the whole creation, as God's purposes unfold themselves. The Stations of the Cross constitute just one of many ways in which we can become better equipped to help forward and co-operate with God's saving work in the world.

Thus, although our journey has taken us along the way of the cross, its end is forward-looking and hopeful. The old *Via dolorosa* in Jerusalem actually ends within the Church of the Holy Sepulchre, which the Greeks prefer to call the Church of the Resurrection. To share in Christ's passion is to share in his rising, and the early Fathers of the Church were correct in interpreting the passion of our Lord as the victory which liberates the world and makes possible a fuller life for the race of men. So we can say: 'We adore thee, O Christ, and we bless thee, because by the holy cross thou hast redeemed the world!' But this mysterious saving power of the cross we could never know so long as we regard the event of Calvary only from the outside, as a fact of history or a doctrine of atonement or whatever. From that point of view, it is foolishness. We know it only through our participation in it.

The Reconciliation of a Penitent

Forgiveness and reconciliation have a central place in the Christian gospel. In Jesus's own ministry, a pronouncement of the forgiveness of sin might accompany an act of healing, as in the case of the paralytic (Mark 2.2–12); at the crucifixion he prays for the forgiveness of his enemies (Luke 23.24); he had already at the Last Supper said that the shedding of his blood was for the forgiveness of sins (Matt. 26.28). He encouraged human beings to forgive one another and linked this to the forgiveness that they might expect of God, as in the Lord's Prayer (Matt. 7.12); or the need to be reconciled to the neighbour before bringing a gift to the altar (Matt. 5.23); or as in the story of the unmerciful debtor (Matt. 18.23–25). There is no limit to such forgiveness – it is demanded not seven times but seventy times seven (Matt. 18.22). The Gospels also attest that Christ committed a ministry of forgiveness to his followers. The traditional Anglican ordinal gave great prominence to the words addressed by the risen Christ to the disciples gathered together on the evening of Easter Day: 'If you forgive the sins of any, they are forgiven; if you retain the sins of any, they are retained' (John 20.23). Matthew's Gospel, which, as it already apparent from this paragraph, has a special concern with forgiveness, records the controversial words addressed to Peter: 'I will give you the keys of the kingdom of heaven, and whatever you bind on earth shall be bound in heaven, and whatever you loose on earth shall be loosed in heaven' (Matt. 16.19). Paul can sum up the Christian ministry as 'the ministry of reconciliation' and claims that it has been given by Christ himself (II Cor. 5.18–19).

In view of the evidence, there would surely be general agreement that forgiveness of sins is central to the Christian message, that reconciliation to God goes hand in hand with reconciliation to one's fellow human beings, and that a ministry of reconciliation has been entrusted to the Church. This, however, is still very far from establishing a specifically sacramental or quasi-sacramental rite for the reconciliation of a penitent. Or, to speak more accurately, if such a rite was implied, then it was baptism. It is probable that the summons to repentance in the New Testament and the language about binding and loosing – language borrowed from Judaism – refer to baptism, which was the royal way from man's fallen state to reconciliation with God and to the risen life in Christ. Participation in the Eucharist was also a way to reconciliation and, more generally, the preaching and hearing of the gospel was a vehicle of forgiveness and reconciliation.

There are some other passages in the New Testament which complicate the situation somewhat. In the epistle of James, Christians are enjoined to confess their sins to one another (James 5.16). Presumably these are post-baptismal sins. Again, in Matthew's Gospel, where there is already a developed concept of the Church, we read that someone who had sinned might be confronted privately with his fault by another member of the Church. If this achieved nothing, he might be reported to the congregation, and if he remained intransigent, he could be cut off from the fellowship (Matt. 18.15–18). This is an example of 'binding and loosing'. We have also to remember that, according to the form critics, incidents or sayings related to Jesus in the Gospels may reflect problems in the nascent Church. We have already noted Jesus's assurance to the paralytic, 'My son, your sins are forgiven' (Mark 2.5). The scribes objected to these words, even saying they were blasphemous. According to Bultmann, this incident reflects a controversy between the infant Church and the synagogue. The Church, he says, believed that it had received from Christ both the power to heal and the closely related power to forgive sin, and 'demonstrates by her possession of healing powers that she has the right to forgive sins'.[1]

The scattered indications mentioned in the preceding paragraph, though still far from the sacrament of reconciliation as understood and practised in later times, nevertheless open certain possibilities of development. We have to ask how this development came about, and to what extent it may be regarded as a legitimate development within the life of the Church from the scriptural teaching about forgiveness of sins. One factor above all influenced this development, just as it influenced so many others. That one factor was, of course, the fading of the intense eschatological expectations which had been there at the birth of Christianity. As the years passed and the end of the age still did not come, Christians had to reassess many questions and make readjustments. While the end was supposed to be very close and the present age was passing away, everything had a provisional character. There was no point in making arrangements for the future, for the time before the return of the Lord was very short. But when it became apparent that the end might be indefinitely delayed and that possibly a very long future lay ahead of the Christian community, the whole self-understanding of that community had to change. Many matters which had hitherto been left indeterminate or variable had to be regulated and institutionalized, for only so can a continuing historical community survive and maintain its identity. Thus, for instance, the distinctive shape of the ordained ministry began to emerge at this time.

The first generation of Christians may well have believed that the end of the age would come while they were still alive. But if people were going to live many years after baptism and if entire generations were to be born, live and die before the end of the age, then what was to be done about sins committed after baptism? What was to be done, for instance, with a man who lapsed from the Church in a time of persecution, and then sought to be restored? Already in the sub-apostolic writing known as *The Shepherd of Hermas*, dated to the first half of the second century and regarded in some of the early churches as canonical, this question is faced and answered. It is first of all stated that 'he who has received remission of his sins (in baptism) ought not to sin any more, but to live in purity'. But it is recognized that human nature is weak, and God in his mercy permits a subsequent repentance. But this can be on one occasion only, and any subsequent repentances will be of no avail.[2] Though practice varied from place to place, the possibility of one repentance after baptism came to be generally accepted. The bishop rather than any fellow Christian was the agent of reconciliation, and there was some public act of penance, though it was always clear that this did not earn forgiveness but was rather a token and manifestation of the change of heart. We can already discern in these early practices the main outlines of the later sacrament of penance. The Church rejected the extreme rigorism of those who would allow no further opportunity for repentance after baptism, yet by its rule of 'once only' did not allow the reconciliation of a penitent to become merely a routine matter. Furthermore, by insisting on public penance, the penitent was not easily let off the hook. As one theologian has remarked, 'The lot of the penitents was not a happy one, nor was it meant to be'.[3] Of course, in those days preparation for baptism was also a very strenuous and demanding matter.

There are many histories of the ministration of reconciliation in the Church, and no attempt will be made to rehearse that history here. But it may be said that the early tension between rigorists on the one side and laxists (or, perhaps one should say, people of more moderate views) on the other has continued, and is perhaps still with us, as can be seen in recent arguments about so-called 'indiscriminate' baptism. As far as the sacrament of reconciliation is concerned, the discomforts and humiliations which had attended it in the early centuries were in the main relaxed. Confession became a private matter between the penitent and his priest, and penances likewise were privatized and reduced usually to reciting a psalm or something of the sort. Among the rival schools of casuistry, it was the relatively permissive probabilism which prevailed over more rigorous viewpoints. Thus in course of time both baptism and the rite of reconciliation (and we have seen that the two are closely linked) tended to lose their seriousness and to become matters of routine.

Such was the state of affairs at the time of the Reformation when the sacrament of penance in the form which it had developed in the Middle Ages virtually disappeared among Protestants. Luther indeed continued to value it, though with some ambivalence, but it is interesting to note that some Lutherans have continued to attach importance to a sacramental form of confession and absolution, especially Dietrich Bon-hoeffer, who testifies to the value of the practice in the underground seminary which he operated in Germany at the time of the Hitler regime.[4] The Calvinist churches, with their opposition to prelacy and clericalism, did not provide for auri-cular confession, but they did, presumably on their interpreta-tion of Matt. 18.15–18, encourage both ministers and elders to examine the lives both of the people and of each other, and quite severe disciplinary measures were taken where it was thought appropriate.[5]

In the Church of England no specific liturgical form for the reconciliation of a penitent was included in the Prayer Book, but from the first book of 1549 onwards, provision for such an act of reconciliation is made for certain special occasions. Such an occasion is preparation for receiving communion, where the person concerned 'needs further comfort or counsel' to quiet his conscience; another occasion is provided in the office for the visitation of the sick. On the other hand, successive editions of the Prayer Book made plentiful provision (some have thought, too much) for penitential acts consisting of a general confession, followed by an absolution pronounced by the priest. For a long time this remained the general Anglican practice, with sacra-mental or quasi-sacramental reconciliation of individual peni-tents taking place only on rather exceptional occasions. But the aftermath of the Oxford Movement brought with it a revival of the sacrament of penance – a revival which was accompanied by a good deal of controversy. In the absence of any specific Anglican liturgical form, it was usual to make use of the form current in the Roman Catholic Church. In course of time, a considerable number of Anglicans came to accept regular resort to the sacrament of reconciliation as a valued part of their Christian discipleship. The commonest practice has been to make confession and receive absolution perhaps three or four times a year, especially before the great festivals, and those who follow such a practice attest that to hear and inwardly appro-priate the words, 'Your sins are forgiven!' deepens the joy and significance of participation in the festival. But with the typical Anglican respect for freedom of conscience, no pressure is put on anyone as to the manner, still less the frequency, with which reconciliation is to be restored or quickened. As has often been wisely said about this matter, 'All may; none must; some should'.

Now that the practice of making confession and hearing absolution is so widespread in the Anglican Communion, it is natural that thought should be given to drawing up an appropriate liturgical form. This is particularly desirable because the Roman Catholic Church has itself been engaged is revising the rite which Anglicans borrowed in the past. The Episcopal Church in the United States has already taken a lead and included in its new edition of the Prayer Book a form for the reconciliation of a penitent. Strictly speaking, it has included two forms. The first is a fairly conservative revision of the traditional Roman rite. The second is perhaps needlessly elaborate in its language. Both forms provide an alternative absolution which may be used by a lay person, reminding us that, to begin with, a confession might be made to any fellow Christian, a point which continued to be recognized in the Roman Catholic Church where, in the penitential introduction to the Mass, the celebrant and servers made confessions of sin to each other, and were in turn prayed for.

A few points may be made about the various parts which make up the office for the reconciliation of a penitent.

(i) The confession made by the penitent, after some brief introductory phrase, such as 'Bless me, for I have sinned'. This confession may very well take the form, already familiar to the penitent, of one of the general confessions used in the services of the Church of England, with the insertion at an appropriate point of the particular sins which are weighing on the conscience of the penitent. However, I would avoid the use of the general confession which stands near the beginning of Rite A and which says 'we have sinned against you and against our fellow men'. 'Sin' is a specifically theological word, and refers to our defiance of God. It is a misuse of language to talk about sinning against our fellow men or women. We harm them, offend against them, etc., and all this is at the same time a sin against God, but it is against God only that (in the strict sense of the word) we sin. Thus the alternative form of confession (B) given in section 80 is preferable, suitably modified for a private and particular rather than a general confession.

(ii) Having heard the confession, the priest normally offers some words of counsel and encouragement. Strictly speaking, this is not part of the essence of the rite. Counsel may be asked for and given quite apart from a sacramental act of reconciliation. But this pastoral element is important for forming a continuing relation between the hearer of the confession and the penitent, the bond which we call 'spiritual direction' and which, in the case of a wise counsellor, can be very powerful in building up individuals in the Christian life.

(iii) At this point, the priest also asks the penitent to perform some act as a practical expression of his penitence. As was said above, this is in no sense a way of 'earning' forgiveness. Neither penitence itself nor any of its expressions is a 'work', but only our response to the proclamation of God's gracious forgiveness. We have to give thought to the question of what kind of penance is appropriate, and this would take account of the individual concerned. Just to tell everyone to read such and such a psalm, for instance, could be too mechanical and even trivial. Perhaps a penitent priest could be told to go and spend several hours studying a part of the Bible or some book that could make his ministry more effective.

(iv) There has been some controversy over the form of absolution. It is customary to distinguish three forms of absolution, and all three occur in the Book of Common Prayer. The precatory form is a prayer that God will forgive the penitent – this is the form that has been traditionally used and is still used in the Holy Communion. The declaratory form, used at Morning and Evening Prayer in 1662 (but not in ASB), is a straightforward declaration to the people, 'being penitent', that God pardons and absolves them. The indicative form, found in the Visitation of the Sick, uses the expression 'I absolve you in the name of the Father and the Son and the Holy Spirit'. It is over this last form that there has been disagreement, some feeling that it is too sacerdotal and seems to arrogate to the priest a power which belongs only to God. Attempts have been made to devise other forms of absolution which would somehow bring together the different forms. I am bound to say that I think this controversy has no real substance to it. There is surely no *theological* difference among the various forms of absolution. They are different verbal formulations of the one fundamental communication – that God, the Father of our Lord Jesus Christ, desires life and not death for his creatures, and has forgiven the penitent, and this forgiveness is now declared to him by an appointed and authorized minister of the Church. If we study the formulae closely, we shall discover that they all say the same. Though the priest may use the words 'I absolve you', the language makes it quite clear that he does this only in the name of God and by the commandment given to him to announce the forgiveness of sins. We have already seen many parallels between the reconciliation of a penitent and baptism. In the baptismal service, the form of words is 'I baptize you in the name of the Father and of the Son and of the Holy Spirit'. No one supposes that this is an arrogant sacerdotalism, and no other forms are used in the Western churches. It is understood that in every sacrament or sacramental act it is the divine agency that is the true agency, though making use of the agency of the human minister. Perhaps the solution to this pseudo-problem is simply to say that the priest shall pronounce absolution using one of the forms customary in this Church.

It was noted that in the American Church two complete rites for the reconciliation of a penitent are offered. But both of them have in mind the private confessions of individuals. Roman Catholics have been more adventurous in seeking to make the sacrament of reconciliation (as they generally call it nowadays) less individualistic. It has been suggested that on certain occasions, such as Shrove Tuesday, there could be a corporate act of penitence. Then individuals could go privately to make their special confessions. Finally, all would return for a corporate assurance of forgiveness and an act of thanksgiving. I hope the Church of England might be thinking also along these lines, as well as providing forms for the reconciliation of individuals.[6]

XIV

Rest and Restlessness in Christian Spirituality

The ancient city of Basel possesses a beautiful minster, standing high above the Rhine on a site where Christian worship has been offered continuously since about the year 800. Basel's reformer, Oecolampadius, was a humanist, and so the minster's statues, monuments and carvings were largely spared at the time when iconoclasts were busy elsewhere. But one curious modification did occur. On the west front of the minster, on the north side of the great door, can be seen St George on horseback, thrusting his spear into the dragon. On the south side of the door is another horseman, but he is in isolation, and one feels that something is missing. In fact, this other horseman is St Martin, and originally the group was balanced by the figure of the beggar to whom St Martin gave his cloak. But at the time of the Reformation, the beggar was removed. The reasoning was that this public display of St Martin performing a meritorious act might lead the people to the mistaken belief that they could gain salvation through good works. So for the past four hundred years, St Martin has been riding on by himself, doing nothing at all. And this *dolce far niente* proclaims for all who can understand such matters the glorious truth of *sola gratia* – that we are saved by grace alone, and not through works.

Nowadays when we hear this little story we find it rather amusing. Nevertheless, it draws our attention to two important facts about our Christian religion. The first is that in matters both of faith and practice we find ourselves in a tension of opposites, so that we have to live and believe dialectically, not letting go either side but recognizing that both have just claims upon us. For instance, in matters of faith, we have to acknowledge that God is transcendent and yet he is immanent, that he is one and yet he is three, that our Lord Jesus Christ is divine and yet he is human, that he is the eternal Word and yet that he was born and lived on this earth at a particular time in history; and so we could go on. Likewise, in matters of practice, we have to acknowledge the apparently conflicting claims of contemplation and action, of worship and service to others, of private morality and commitment to social or political ideals – and again we could go on listing the contrasts. The second fact is that when placed in this dialectical situation, neither the Church as a whole nor individual Christians have been notably successful in facing up to the total demand in all its complexity. Usually the tension has been relaxed, and some one-sided simplistic solution has been adopted, as happened in the case of those Basel reformers who thought that the sovereignty of the divine grace could be safeguarded only by discouraging good works.

Of course, in any given situation, one side or other of the dialectic may need to be emphasized to make up for earlier neglect. Some exaggeration seems inevitable, and if one were ever to reach a state of equilibrium, this might well turn out to be a kind of death, in which the dynamic had gone out of Christianity and further advance had become impossible. But it is quite another matter to so exaggerate one side of the dialectic that one becomes almost totally insensitive to the other. But this is what often happens in the history of the Church – the so-called swing of the pendulum. A truly catholic theology and spirituality try to maintain the wholeness of the Christian heritage, while freely acknowledging that different items in that heritage may need to be stressed at different times.

It is a curious irony that the Protestant thrust, which went to such exaggerated lengths at the time of the Reformation in stressing the *sola fide* principle and in correspondingly de-emphasizing good works, has in our own day gone to the opposite extreme, for now we hear of nothing but activism and involvement in public affairs. The most shattering indictment of this new onesidedness has come from a distinguished theologian in the Reformed tradition, Professor Thomas F. Torrance of Edinburgh. He sees 'the vast slide of Church leaders in recent times into something like an obsession with socio-moral concerns' and their desire for 'consciously meritorious involvement in socio-political issues' as concomitant with a decay of the inward substance of faith and so with a need for self-justification. Professor Torrance goes on: 'I am more and more staggered at two things: first, the astonishing *volte-face* that has been taking place in the Churches of the Reformation, in that they reveal a serious lapse from the centrality of the gospel of Christ, together with a failure to understand that it is justification by grace alone which creates the ethical disturbance that turns the world upside down; and, secondly, the growing contradiction that the Western Churches exhibit to Jesus' total rejection of every value system based on power, and his proclamation of the new order, which cannot be brought about by any form of force, together with a failure to remember that Jesus was crucified by contemporaries who bitterly resented his refusal to have anything whatsoever to do with their political theology.'[1] Of course, the prevailing drive toward justification by works is not confined to the Protestant Churches, but has many sympathizers among Roman Catholics.

The tendencies described are to be seen in Churches all over the world, but they seem to have assumed a particularly acute form in the American Churches. Pragmatism has for long been a powerful force in the United States, and ideas are valued to the extent that they can be set to work. On the other hand, anything savouring of quietism has been suspect.

But must we always be blown about by extremes of doctrine and practice? Can we not learn to become at once more dialectical and more catholic? Is it so very difficult to entertain more than one idea at a time? Has Anglicanism, traditionally the *via media*, something to teach the other branches of the Christian Church on these matters? And if we have to emphasize one element of truth more than another, is it not more important to acknowledge our receptiveness in the presence of God than our own doing?

These questions bring me to the particular contrast which forms the theme of this essay – rest and restlessness in the Christian life. They lead me also at this point to acknowledge my debt to Canon Edward West, in whose honour this essay was originally written. At the time when I was preparing for ordination to the priesthood, Canon West was my guide and counsellor on all questions relating to prayer, liturgy and spirituality. He even entrusted me with the loan of his own personally annotated prayer book. There can be very few people in the Anglican Communion who approached Canon West in his profound knowledge and understanding of these matters. So often, too, those who are deemed 'knowledgable' in liturgy and spirituality are found to be conversant with the history of the subject, possibly even in great detail, but to have little understanding for the theological issues and for what one might call more broadly the philosophy of worship. Canon West knew the history but equally he understood the principles. For this reason, he was able to explain to me in a way that made a great deal of sense the ideas underlying the movement for liturgical renewal. Yet just because he understood and sympathized with the true motives of the liturgical reformers, he was also aware of the distortions and exaggerations that have come about where new practices have been adopted without a genuine understanding of their purpose. I remember that on one occasion when he had been talking about liturgical reform, he paused for a moment and said: 'But it can all become very Pelagian.' That remark surely goes to the very heart of the matter.

Rest and restlessness, contemplation and action, prayer and service, grace and works, serenity and concern – all of these have their place in Christian life and spirituality, yet they are always in tension, and it is never easy to order the priorities. To be sure, we have to think in terms that go beyond individual experience, and remembering that the Church is a corporate entity in which different members do different things, we can acknowledge that some by temperament and calling fulfil their discipleship chiefly in the contemplative life, others in the life of action. Yet when this has been said, it does not take away the problem for the individual. Everyone's Christian discipleship needs some balance if it is not to become a distorted caricature. Each one of us has to learn to strike somehow the balance between the apparently equally valid claims of contemplation and action.

For what religion worthy of the name does not hold out to its devotees the promise of rest, peace and serenity? Herein lies much of the appeal of religion. We are finite creatures, largely at the mercy of circumstances over which we have little control. We are harassed by the continual threats that attend our transient mode of existence. Amid all these threats, we long to be able to cling to a rock that is higher than ourselves, to experience an inward tranquility and assurance that will give the lie to all the appearances of evil in the world. Is it just weakness that stirs such a desire in us? Or is it part of the meaning of finitude that we must look beyond ourselves and seek a ground on which we can rest? Christianity has never been ashamed of responding to this cry of the human heart. Our Lord himself told his disciples that his parting gift to them was peace. For centuries, Christian devotion has talked of resting in Jesus, of casting care upon him and so on. All this constitutes, at the very least, an ineluctable part of Christian spiritual history. If this is weakness and neurosis, so be it – but there is no way that it can be dissociated from the Christian tradition. And is it not the case that the Christians who impress us most deeply are precisely those who have developed a certain serenity and inner quiet, so that they can give us confidence when we turn to them? To whom do we go for counsel when we are at our wit's end and the world is falling to pieces around us? We go, as likely as not, to someone who has been formed in what we call the religious life. His mind we find to be like a sacred space where wisdom and sanity still prevail and the madness of the world has not penetrated. And we turn to such Christians because we believe that through their spiritual discipline they have become in some measure like God. Every man and woman is made in the image of God, and Christian discipleship consists in strengthening and developing that image through conforming us to Christ, who is the express image of God in a human existence. We cannot speak of God unless there is a real sense in which God endures unchanging through the changes and chances that beset our earthly existence. Part of the meaning of the very word 'God' is that it denotes one whose being is like an infinite calm transcending the storms of time and history. And the end of the Christian life has also been visualized in terms of rest. '*Requiem aeternam dona eis. . . .*' Our prayer is that the departed, after all the pains and struggles of their life on earth, may attain to the vision of God and to participation in his life, and so to the peace that passes understanding. And we believe that even now, in the midst of the struggle, in moments of intense awareness of God, we glimpse the vision and know the peace and enjoy, as it were, a corner of heaven on earth.

All I have said about rest and peace in that long paragraph is true. And yet, as soon as it has been said, we recognize that almost every point needs to be qualified by saying something else which seems to contradict it, but seems, nevertheless, to be equally true. Granted that Christianity, like every religion, offers peace, we have still to ask, 'What kind of peace?' There is a hymn familiar to American church people that turns it all around, and suggests that before the coming of Christ among them, the first Galilean disciples were simple, happy contented folk. 'The peace of God, it is no peace, but strife closed in the sod.'[2] And now we have to remember that although Christ promised the gift of peace to his followers, he told them also that for his sake they would have to undergo strife and tribulation. So when we talk of rest or peace or serenity as belonging to the essence of Christianity, we can never mean a rest that is just content with things as they are or a peace that means dropping out from the real world and its problems. And when we think more deeply of God himself, although we could not go back on the belief that it is of the very nature of God to transcend the storms that beset finite existence, we must also say that it is of the very nature of the God we have known in Jesus Christ to be alongside his creatures in their suffering. His impassibility could never be understood in any way that would make him an 'apathetic' God, in the modern sense of that adjective. This God of infinite calm and rest is at the same time the God who grieves for his children and yearns for them. And finally, though the end of the Christian life is rest in God, this cannot be a rest in which nothing further will ever happen – that would be a kind of death. Rather, as a great master of the spiritual life, St Gregory of Nyssa, taught, the very perfection of the Christian life is a never-ending advance into the inexhaustible riches of God.

There are the two sides of the truth of rest and restlessness. I doubt if we can synthesize them into a greater, comprehensive truth. Perhaps that kind of understanding is reserved to God alone, or to ourselves only when we have come much nearer to God than we ever are *in via*. For the present, we can only hope to be sensitive to both sides of the truth, and to respond to all its dimensions. Again, if we remember individual differences, we shall not all respond in the same way. We must avoid the temptation to decry the person who responds differently, or to think that our way is the better way, still less the only way. The activist is sadly in error when he despises the man or woman who spends a large part of his time at prayer or in church, and the most obvious proof of this is the fact noted above, that people in trouble turn for help to those whose inner serenity makes it plain that their lives are rooted in a reality deeper than the flux of everyday events. But the contemplative spirit may be equally in error if he censors the activist for being rarely in church or engaged in formal prayer, though he may be very fully engaged in the Lord's business. However, it is perhaps again significant that contemplatives are much less frequently censorious than are activists, for it is part of their wisdom to have a broad compassionate grasp of the endless varieties of human nature.

Still, if the trend at present is in the direction of activism and restlessness, there is a special duty to consider again the claims of contemplation and the value of rest. We now turn to such a consideration, and we shall carry it out in three stages, beginning from a broad perspective and then narrowing down to some of the matters that lie at the centre.

We begin then with the broad perspective, and ask in a general way about the place of prayer and worship in the life of the ordinary Christian. What time ought he to give to them? What priority ought he to accord to them? How are the claims for time of prayer and worship to be reconciled with the claims of action? Such questions have been raised in a somewhat aggressive way in recent years, and although we do not hear as much as we did about a so-called secular Christianity, many people do seem to believe that Christianity consists primarily in good works, and that the rest is a kind of spiritual luxury, and one that we ought to do without in days when there is so much to be done in service to mankind.

In the first place, I think we must get away from any idea that our time and our loyalty are somehow to be 'divided' between competing claims. Just to recall for a moment the New Testament witness, we see our Lord working to the point of physical exhaustion among the people, and we see him retiring into desert places to recollect himself in quiet, but there is no question of any conflict between these two aspects of his ministry. They constitute an undivided whole. So too it ought to be in the lives of his followers. The cultivation of the life of the spirit is not a turning away from the demands and challenges of the active life. The two are continuous. I like to use the word 'concentration' to point to what prayer and worship bring about. These are times when we bring to explicit awareness that relation to Jesus Christ that is present all the time. In this sense, we could describe these as times of consciousness-raising, to use a popular expression. They do not introduce something different, but they concentrate in its intensity that orientation to Jesus Christ present in a diffuse way throughout the whole of the disciple's living and acting. Those theologians who urge us to see God in the neighbour and in the everyday situations of life are perfectly correct in what they affirm – indeed, they are simply commending what has been traditionally called 'habitual recollection', which means living all the time in the presence of God. But some of them feel that they also have to decry the special times of prayer and the special religious occasions, and they are mistaken in what they deny, for I do not think that one can recognize God in the ordinary situations where he is veiled unless one has first learned to know him in those situations where we stand before him in the revealing moment of word or sacrament or prayer. Habitual recollection comes only after one has submitted to the disciplines of the spiritual life.

In the second place, those who would devalue prayer and worship seem to imagine that the Christian life is far easier than it actually is. Perhaps they themselves are *naturaliter Christiani*, and find it no trouble to give themselves in love to the neighbour or to be men and women for others. But I suspect that with most people it is very different. There is less emphasis in Christian theology today on sin than there was in the generation of Reinhold Niebuhr and Karl Barth, but sin has not gone away. Nations, individuals, social classes, racial and ethnic blocs, economic groups – all of these today display just as much hardness and self-interest as ever they did. Christianity does not come easily to any of them. The idea that one can just go out and love one's neighbour is incredibly naïve, and it has not even yet begun to consider what love is – and surely there is no more abused word in the language than this word 'love'. The meaning of love and still more the doing of it have to be learned or, better, received, before we can become agents of love. As Tom Torrance pointed out in the passage quoted earlier, there has to take place the radical disturbance or displacement of grace if the Christian ethic of love is to be released into the world. Let me say again, however, that there must be no division, not even a division into cause and effect. The relation of grace and ethic, of prayer and act, is a reciprocal one. It is knowledge of God in Christ and daily communing with him that sensitizes one for the ordinary situations of life; but on the other hand, these ordinary situations lead into a deeper existential knowledge of God in Christ. To put it in another way, if we have spent time reading the Bible, we shall be better able to respond with compassion and understanding to the current human situations as we find it set forth in today's *Independent* or *New York Times*; but it will be that concrete human situation that will bring alive for us the Bible's teaching.

Advocates of secular Christianity often appeal to the example of Dietrich Bonhoeffer on the basis of some rather obscure passages in his letters, but I think that in fact he illustrates much more convincingly that reciprocity of prayer and action, of rest and restlessness, which I am commending here. Dr Michael Ramsey has given careful consideration to those passages in Bonhoeffer's letters which support the idea of a 'religionless' Christianity, and in response to the question whether these passages can really be held to represent Bonhoeffer's mind on the matter, Dr Ramsey says this: 'My own answer is found largely in many other passages in Bonhoeffer's *Letters and Papers from Prison*, and reading the letters as a whole, I find two things vividly impressed me. First, that God is found in the tragedy of the world, far outside the religious camp. Second, that for all Bonhoeffer says about religion, religion is growing powerfully in his own soul. Again and again in his letters, he is expressing his dependence upon God through the medium of his own memory of hymns and psalms and music, the rhythms of the Christian year, the stuff of the worshipping tradition.' Dr Ramsey quotes extensively from the letters to support his point, and draws attention to 'the submissiveness which is the mark of the religious man'. But he pushes the matter further: 'Is this religious element so strongly present in Bonhoeffer's letters a kind of hangover from that immaturity from which, he says, the Christian must move onwards? No, the religion disclosed in the letters seems to me far from retrogressive. Rather does it seem to mount from strength to strength.'[3] One might add to Dr Ramsey's testimony that of the camp doctor who was present at Bonhoeffer's execution: 'Through the half-open door in one room of the huts I saw Pastor Bonhoeffer, before taking off his prison garb, kneeling on the floor praying fervently to his God. I was most deeply moved by the way this lovable man prayed, so devout and so certain that God heard his prayer. . . . In the almost fifty years that I worked as a doctor, I have hardly ever seen a man die so entirely submissive to the will of God.'[4]

Bonhoeffer's prayer, we may say, concentrated his life of discipleship, but his life gave expression to his prayer. Neither is conceivable without the other, and it is this relationship of inward submission to and rest in God with outward action in God's service that each Christian must work out in his own life in the way that will best fulfil his own discipleship.

Now we must narrow the range of our consideration. If we have established that in the Christian life there is a place for simply resting in God, for resorting to him in prayer and adoration (though this will not be isolated from the remainder of our concerns), we have still to ask about the structure of this specifically spiritual discipline itself. Traditionally, it included both participation in the public liturgy and such private acts of prayer and devotion as each person might find suited to his or her needs. But today there is strong pressure against what might be called the private sector of spirituality. And again it is the activist spirit that is exerting this pressure. The attitude seems to be: 'If it has to be acknowledged that some prayer and worship are needed in the Christian life, then let us indeed make eucharist together as a corporate act, but then let us immediately return to the world and its service.' Thus, whereas people used to remain kneeling in prayer for a little while after, they are now urged to leave with instant abruptness. 'Go, the mass is over!' is interpreted with a literalness that hardly encourages us to see a continuity between the Eucharist and life outside the sanctuary. Again, whereas the Eucharist used to be the centre around which there was a whole structure of offices and devotions, the tendency now is to discourage any acts of prayer and worship apart from the Eucharist itself.

Of course, one cannot deny the element of truth in the current tendencies. The Eucharist is the centre and model for all Christian spirituality, and its restoration to the central place is one of the great achievements of recent times. In the Roman Catholic Church, the Eucharist until recently was frequently smothered in the plethora of private devotions that had grown up around it. In the Anglican Communion and most of the Protestant Churches, the Eucharist was often displaced by a service of the word alone. Certainly, no one can complain that eucharistic worship has been gaining ground on all sides – rather one must warmly welcome this. But again, it is not what is affirmed that causes concern, but what is denied. Can the Eucharist be exalted only by a devaluing of the office, devotions to the Blessed Sacrament reserved, the rosary and all the other forms of prayer that have been found helpful in the life of the Christian – precisely the forms, be it noted, which encourage the contemplative and meditative aspects of spirituality?

Thomas Merton, who in a remarkable way combined the contemplative and the active modes of life, stated bluntly: 'The true fruition of the eucharist is not normally possible unless our eucharistic communion is somehow prolonged in silent and solitary adoration.'[5] This is the other side of the truth, which must also be maintained in spite of all the pressures against it at the present time. We shall not 'get it right', so to speak, if rest is completely swallowed up in restlessness. Dr Hans Urs von Balthasar has put it very well: 'One sees clearly where things had got on to the wrong track: the event became static, the process became a state, that which offered itself incomprehensibly became that which was offered in graspable form, that which transcended sight became that which was seen, the presence of the divine was turned into an earthly presence. All that sounds plausible. But perhaps, if we think it through more deeply, we shall not be able to bring it down to such simple formulae.'[6] We hear in these words the true dialectic of Christian truth and Christian life, and we need to hear these words if we are to be delivered from the impoverishment that comes from onesidedness and oversimplification. Let us by all means ensure the centrality of the Eucharist, but let us not fail to provide such other occasions of prayer and devotion as will help to extend the meaning of the Eucharist into every area of life, through our profound meditation on its mysteries.

If then we have established that there is a place for appropriate acts of devotion alongside the Eucharist, let us come to the final focusing of our perspective, namely, on the Eucharist itself. There are many dimensions to this great Christian sacrament, and at different times in history or in different traditions of Christendom, different dimensions of the sacrament have been stressed. In our own time, the stress has come to be on what we call the 'horizontal' dimension, that is to say, the sacrament seen as a common meal in which is both expressed and realized the solidarity of believers in the body of Christ. This is a true and essential part of the meaning of the Eucharist, and no doubt it needed to be reasserted, for in all Christian traditions the nature of the Eucharist as a ruly corporate action had become obscured. But once again it is important to affirm without denying, to lay hold on the new (or newly rediscovered) enrichment without becoming insensitive to what we have known hitherto. For without its 'vertical' dimension, the relation to the transcendent God, the Eucharist is emptied of its power and significance.

Once more, however, it is important to see that there cannot be a rivalry here. We cannot honour God unless we are in love and charity with our neighbours; but we cannot love our neighbours as we ought unless we are lifted out of ourselves and set in orbit around God. If this essential vertical dimension is to come through clearly in our eucharistic celebrations, then we have to think again about what is happening in liturgical reform. The movement has been all in one direction. The use of informal language, the westward position of the celebrant, the elimination of the moments of penitence and humility, the prominence given to the kiss of peace and to communion as over against consecration and oblation – all these taken together have produced a massive shift in the meaning of the sacrament. There is no one of these points that cannot be defended, and perhaps no one of them has not been needed to correct earlier exaggerations. But there is no doubt that the total effect has been to let the Eucharist appear chiefly as something that is going on among ourselves and that we are doing for ourselves, with God kept discreetly in the background. In this sense, Edward West's comment about Pelagianism was well taken. It is time that we gave thought to changing direction in our liturgical thinking, and to making clear that above all it is God in Christ who founds and initiates the sacramental action. And this can only be done if we find room in our rites for rest as well as action, for moments of quiet, passivity, receptiveness, humility, adoration before the mystery of the God who reaches out to us before we ever dream of turning to him and before we ever learn rightly to love each other.

Rest and restlessness both have their place in the Christian life. But of late we have had too much of the restlessness, and surely the time has come for us to learn again the value of being quietly open to God.

XV

Learning to See

In the foregoing chapters there have been set forth the elements of a spirituality which has consciously tried to respond to whatever is valid in the modern critique of religion. We have kept in view the guidelines announced at the beginning,[1] and have understood spirituality as the perfecting of personal being, as forward-looking and dynamic, as related to life and action though not absorbed in them, and as aiming at corporate rather than only an individual wholeness. Since this book is concerned with Christian spirituality, we have discussed especially the traditional forms of Christian worship and above all the Eucharist, without which any Christian spirituality is unimaginable. Properly understood and interpreted, these traditional forms are seen to be still fruitful ways whereby man's spirit can come to fulfilment. They speak of a transcendent presence, and mediate that presence through down-to-earth realities; and because of the constant link between Word and Sacrament in Christian spirituality, they stand opposed to any merely emotive 'celebration' which can be as insensitive as it is irrational.

Yet in the very unfolding of this Christian sacramental spirituality, the whole problem of spirituality in the contemporary world has been sharpened. The traditional Christian forms would not have been in need of so much explanation and interpretation if they had not become, as it were, shop-soiled. But it has been their fate to become flattened, conventionalized, distorted, so that even all the efforts for liturgical renewal have had only moderate success in recovering the true meaning of Christian worship in its fulness.

In the past, when the presence of God was obscured in conventionalized ecclesiastical forms of worship, men were often able to realize that presence in nature. But today one would have to say that nature, though in a different way, has become even more shop-soiled than Christian worship. The sky over our metropolitan areas is obscured by smog; the oceans defiled by oil slicks; the countryside littered with rusting remains of automobiles; the streams and lakes rendered dirty and lifeless through industrial effluents, pesticides and the like; the deserts criss-crossed by pipelines. In all of this it has become increasingly hard to recognize a divine presence mediated through the creation.

But the trouble goes deeper still. It is not simply that Christian worship and nature have both, in their several ways, become, as I have said, shop-soiled. Man's own mind has become soiled and insensitive. Of course, human life has always been infected with sin. But Western man has become the prey of a peculiar type of sin. He may infect the rest of mankind, or the rest of mankind may save him. This peculiar type of sin I have called 'the consumer mentality'. For such a mentality, life consists in getting, spending, having. It is an acquisitive mentality and becomes an aggressive mentality, exploiting without responsibility not only nature but other human beings. Yet in this very exploitation those who have such a mentality become themselves diminished in their humanity, for as they are dominated by the endless desire to have and to use and to consume they become less and less persons of freedom and dignity.

The crisis of the West is a spiritual crisis, but it is one of very great complexity. On the one hand, Western technology makes possible for more people than ever before a fuller, better mode of life, for it enables them to enjoy a level of having below which which human freedom and dignity are almost unattainable, because they are crushed out by toil and poverty. On the other hand, the same technology stimulates endless desire for possession and sets up the acquisitive-aggressive syndrome to which I have referred. It is not an accident that we often hear nowadays of the 'military-industrial complex', for in every country the military and industrial aspects of technology are inseparably intertwined.

If the crisis of the West is spiritual, then it has spiritual roots and, if curable at all, must have a spiritual cure. Weber and others, as is well-known, have tried to show a connection between the rise of capitalism and Calvinistic theology. I think this thesis needs to be broadened. Calvinistic theology was only the extreme case of a tendency in all Western theology to exaggerate the transcendence of God to such an extent that the world was conceived as purely external to God, as wholly profane and dedivinized and therefore as entirely given over to human exploitation. This monarchical model of God passed over into the deism of the seventeenth and eighteenth centuries and eventually into practical atheism. The highly exalted God became the distant God and then the absent God. Meanwhile aggressive exploitation of both man and nature grew. 'The spirit of capitalism', wrote Reinhold Niebuhr, 'is the spirit of an irreverent exploitation of nature, conceived as a treasure house of riches which will guarantee everything which might be regarded as the good life.'[2] Incidentally, it is not obvious that socialism is any different from capitalism in this respect. The problem is to get away from the idea that the production and consumption of goods *under any system* is what human life is all about.

But there is surely hope in the restless questing which we see today – questing for a vision of the world in a new wholeness and depth, questing for a larger interpretation of human life that will make room for man's 'sense and taste for the infinite'.[3] And I doubt whether the quest can be fulfilled unless we can realize again the presence of a transcendent Reality that is none the less that which is nearest of all, immanent in the world and in human life itself.

It may be worthwhile recalling the vision of the world and the sense of presence that were once common in the West and are still common in some parts of the world. Then we may ask whether anything of that vision and sense of presence can be made available to those contemporary people who are deficient in them.

I choose as an illustration Celtic spirituality. Although it belongs to a culture that has almost vanished it fulfils in many respects the conditions to which a contemporary spirituality would have to conform. At the very centre of this type of spirituality was an intense sense of presence. The Celt was very much a God-intoxicated man whose life was embraced on all sides by the divine Being. But this presence was always mediated through some finite this-worldly reality, so that it would be difficult to imagine a spirituality more down-to-earth than this one.

The sense of God's immanence in his creation was so strong in Celtic spirituality as to amount sometimes almost to a pantheism. Of course, Celtic Christianity was continuous with the earlier Celtic paganism. The relationship between the two is well symbolized on a notable sculptured stone preserved in Govan church on the Clyde. This stone shows on the one side the sun's disc and on the other the cross. The continuity can be illustrated too from the fact that some of the leading Celtic saints took over the functions and even the names of older pagan deities. The widespread cult of St Brigid, for instance, corresponds to that of a Celtic goddess of the same name.[4] The immanence of God in nature was certainly a strong feature, and no doubt it was easier to believe in that immanence when the world was not yet 'shop-soiled'. But perusal of typical Celtic poems and prayers makes it clear that God's presence was even more keenly felt in the daily round of human tasks and at the important junctures of human life.[5] Getting up, kindling the fire, going to work, going to bed, as well as birth, marriage, settling in a new house, death, were occasions for recognizing the presence of God. All these things could be seen in two ways – as practical occasions to be dealt with, or, in a wider context, as signs of the all-encompassing mystery of God. While I have pointed to the connection with paganism to account for the powerful sense of divine immanence among the Celts, it must also be made clear that their spirituality was in fact christianized. It is strongly trinitarian, and transcendence is combined with immanence. The model for understanding God was the 'High King', but among the Celts the High King was never a remote figure, like an oriental despot or an absolute monarch in European history. The High King of Ireland did in fact have his dwelling on top of the Hill of Tara, but that hill is only a few hundred feet high so that the king was always among his people as well as over them. When God is conceived on such a model, he cannot become too distant and likewise his creation cannot become so profane and godless as to arouse the acquisitive and aggressive spirit of irresponsible concupiscence.

The theology which underlies Celtic spirituality has to be constructed from the implications of the prayers and poems in which that spirituality expressed itself. But some of its most essential features found a more sophisticated expression in recent times in the theology of John Baillie. Though he may not have meant it as a compliment, I think that Ronald Gregor Smith was correct in his judgment when he wrote that 'for all his air of rational caution, John Baillie was a Celtic mystic.'[6] When Baillie argues that God is known as presence rather than by inference, and when he tells us that this presence is a 'mediated immediacy', mediated, that is to say, by persons, things and events within the world, then he is stating in theological language the basic conviction underlying Celtic spirituality. Also, Baillie was one of the few theologians to uphold the doctrine of divine immanence at a time when all the stress was on transcendence. If more attention had been paid to his theology, it might have saved us from some pitfalls and exaggerations.[7]

A great gulf now separates our way of life from that of the Celtic people who practised the presence of God, and perhaps even John Baillie will seem to many old-fashioned. How can one possibly be aware of God's presence in a world that has lost its freshness and been disfigured through overuse? Or how can one see God in the tasks that men perform today, often hurried and routine and apparently lacking that dignity and significance which the Celts saw in their daily round? Are we being asked to make some romantic suspension of disbelief?

I come back to the point made near the beginning of this chapter, and repeat that the greatest obstacle in the way of our realizing the presence of God is not that nature has been subdued and controlled, and not that human society has been transformed radically with the coming of industrialization and urbanization; the greatest obstacle is within ourselves. Our horizons have been narrowed to considerations of production and consumption, our ideal of the good life is built around the advertisements in the glossy magazines, and the only possible result of this unspirituality is an impaired vision.

But we have also seen reason to believe that there are signs of hope in our situation. Many people are searching, and some are finding. Perhaps none have found a fully rounded spirituality, yet in fragmentary ways some are seeing with clarity and in

depth, and they are helping others to see. Let me briefly
mention two men of our own time who have had something of
the vision and sensitivity to presence that was characteristic of
Celtic spirituality, though each of these men exemplifies a
different aspect of it.

The first is Michel Quoist. In describing how the Celts were
conscious of God's presence in their daily occupations, I used
the word 'signs' about these human events. Quoist teaches how
to see the ordinary events of the contemporary world as 'signs'.
They may be events that on the surface seem trivial enough, yet
when they are explored they point beyond themselves to larger
realities and eventually, he believes, to God. This interpretation
of signs – one might almost say, this transignification of everyday
realities – is made possible by living in the reciprocity of the
Christian tradition and the contemporary world. It is, if one
may express it so, an extension of the Eucharist to the events
of human life. 'If only we knew how to look at life . . .
all life would become a sign . . . all of life would become a
prayer.'[8]

Quoist is a master in looking at human life. But human life is
set in a cosmos in which there are vast non-human forces at
work. God must be Lord of all. Is there any possibility in the
modern world of seeing God in nature, in ways that are not
nostalgic or romantic? Here it seems to me that one might set
alongside the spirituality of Quoist that of Teilhard de Chardin.
He looks at nature as one with a scientific understanding, but
again he sees not just isolated facts but signs. 'By virtue of the
Creation and, still more, of the Incarnation, nothing here below
is profane for those who know how to see . . . In the life that
wells up in me and in the matter that sustains me, I find much
more than Your gifts. It is You Yourself whom I find, You who
makes me participate in Your being, You who moulds me.'[9]
Here we come once again on a sense of immanent presence so
intense that it seems to verge on pantheism. But it is more truly
understood as sacramental. He does not hesitate to speak of the
'transubstantiation' of the cosmos as he extends the eucharistic
perspective to the whole of reality: 'In a secondary and general-
ised sense, but in a true sense, the sacramental species are
formed by the totality of the world, and the duration of the
creation is the time needed for its consecration.'[10]

These examples show us that spiritual vision is still possible, and that prayer and worship can still be realities. Without them, human life is impoverished. With them, it moves nearer to that fulness which God intends for it.

Notes

Chapter I

1. Cf. Theodore Roszak, *The Making of a Counter Culture*, London: Faber & Faber 1970.
2. In a lecture at Trinity Institute, New York, in January 1971.
3. See 'The New Rebel Cry: Jesus is Coming!', *Time*, vol. 97, no. 25 (21 June 1971), pp.32–43.
4. J. Deotis Roberts, *Liberation and Reconciliation: A Black Theology*, Philadelphia: Westminster Press 1971, pp.18, 56. Cf. James H. Cone, *Black Power and Black Theology*, New York: Seabury Press 1969, pp.98f.
5. Rubem M. Alves, *A Theology of Human Hope*, Washington: Corpus Books 1969, p.23.
6. See his article, 'For Christ's Sake', *Playboy*, January 1970. His views are more fully developed in *The Feast of Fools*, Cambridge, Mass.: Harvard University Press, and London: OUP 1970.
7. H. H. Price, *Belief*, London: Allen & Unwin 1969, p.475.
8. Michael Novak, *Belief and Unbelief*, London: Darton, Longman & Todd, and New York: Macmillan 1966, p.156.
9. Pierre Teilhard de Chardin, *Le Milieu Divin*, London: Collins (*Divine Milieu*, New York: Harper) 1960, p.118.
10. *Ibid.*
11. Ludwig Feuerbach, *The Essence of Faith according to Luther*, New York: Harper & Row 1967, p.41.
12. F. Schleiermacher, *The Christian Faith*, Edinburgh: T. & T. Clark 1928, pp.589, 674.

Chapter II

1. Eccles. 4.12.
2. L. Wittgenstein, *Philosophical Investigations*, Oxford: Blackwell, and New York: Macmillan 1953, p.11e.
3. Gabriel Moran, FSC, *Theology of Revelation*, New York: Herder & Herder 1966, p.127.
4. James 2.19.
5. W. Rauschenbusch, *A Theology for the Social Gospel*, New York: Macmillan 1918, p.1.
6. *Ibid.*

7. Cf. *Principles of Christian Theology*, London: SCM Press, and New York: Scribner 1966, p.434.

8. 'The Reform of Catholic Liturgy', *Worship*, vol. 41, no. 3 (March 1967), pp.150f.

9. Irenaeus, *Adv. Haer.*, IV, 20.7.

10. Cf. Gal. 1.15–17.

11. I Cor. 9.24–27.

12. Eph. 4.13.

13. Gal. 5.16–6.10.

14. Gal. 6.4f.

15. Cf. I Cor. 7.1–9.

16. *The New Being*, New York: Scribner 1955; London: SCM Press 1956, p.121.

17. See pp. 33–4, 118–19, 158–9.

Chapter III

1. See below, pp.35ff.

2. Iris Murdoch, *The Sovereignty of Good*, London: Routledge & Kegan Paul 1970, p.101.

3. *Belief and Unbelief*, p.107.

4. Marshall McLuhan, *Understanding Media: The Extensions of Man*, New York: New American Library 1964; London: Routledge & Kegan Paul 1965, p.118.

5. *Meister Eckhart: A Modern Translation*, New York: Harper 1941, p.238.

6. D. Hammarskjold, *Markings*, London: Faber & Faber, and New York: Knopf 1964, pp.65, 108.

7. Luke 11.1.

8. See Chapter XII below.

9. Karl Jaspers, *Philosophical Faith and Revelation*, New York: Harper & Row, and London: Collins 1967, p.125.

10. Bernard Häring, *Shalom: Peace*, New York: Farrar, Strauss & Giroux 1968, p.117.

11. Mark Gibbard, SSJE, *Why Pray?* London: SCM Press, and Valley Forge: Judson Press 1970, p.31.

12. Herbert Waddams, *Companion to the Book of Common Prayer*, London: Mowbray 1966, p.32.

13. Haushofer was shot along with Bonhoeffer's brother and brother-in-law. See Eberhard Bethge, *Dietrich Bonhoeffer*, London: Collins, and New York: Harper and Row 1970, p.832.

14. From *Moabiter Sonette*, Berlin: Lothar Blanvalet Verlag 1946. Translation mine.

15. Luke 22.42.

16. Ian Shevill, *Going It – with God*, Sydney; A. H. & A. W. Reed 1968, p.74.

Chapter IV

1. This seems to have been true of a great many languages – not only English but Latin, Greek, Sanskrit, Hebrew and others.

2. W. Eichrodt, *Theology of the Old Testament II*, London: SCM Press, and Philadelphia: Westminster Press 1967, p.46.

3. O. C. Quick, *Doctrines of the Creed*, London: Nisbet, and New York: Scribner 1938, p.275.

4. G. W. F. Hegel, *Logic* from The Encyclopedia of the Philosophical Sciences, Oxford: Clarendon Press 1892, p.180.

5. John 3.8.

6. Eph. 2.18.

7. Rom. 8.15.

8. Gen. 2.7.

9. The word 'ex-ience' is formed in analogy with 'trans-ience' from Latin *ire*, to go.

10. The word 'ec-basis' is formed in analogy with 'ana-basis' from Greek *basis*, a going.

11. Gal. 5.22f. See above, p.17.

12. I Cor. 12.7.

13. John 3.6.

14. John 15.26.

15. C. A. Heurtley, ed., *On Faith and the Creed*, Oxford: Parker 1886, p.172.

16. Dale Moody, *Spirit of the Living God*, Philadelphia: Westminster Press, 1968, p.28.

17. Gen. 1.2.

18. John 3.8.

Chapter V

1. Matt. 16.17.

2. The kind of subjectivism I am criticizing is, of course, quite different from the type of mysticism found in St Augustine and others, in which one returns into the abyss of one's own being in order to be led *beyond* it to the being of God.

3. Joseph Addison, in *The English Hymnal*, No. 511.

4. Alec Vidler, *Twentieth-Century Defenders of the Faith*, London: SCM Press, and New York: Seabury Press 1965, p.116.

5. T. F. Torrance, *God and Rationality*, London: OUP 1971, p.29.

6. See below, p. 63.

7. See below, p. 86.

8. Questions of liturgical renewal are discussed in Chapter VII below.

9. Martin Thornton, *The Rock and the River*, London: Hodder & Stoughton, and New York: Morehouse-Barlow, 1965, p.115.

10. This chapter is a revised version of an address given to the American branch of the Confraternity of the Blessed Sacrament in St Paul's Cathedral, Fond du Lac, Wisconsin.

Chapter VI

1. See above, p. 4.

2. *The Making of a Counter Culture*, pp.145f.

3. Paul Tillich, *Systematic Theology* I, Chicago: University of Chicago Press 1951; London: Nisbet 1953, p.118.

4. *God and Rationality*, p.10.

5. For a full discussion of these questions, see my book *God-Talk*, London: SCM Press, and New York: Harper and Row 1967.

6. Michael Polanyi's *Personal Knowledge* (New York: Harper & Row 1964) remains an outstanding contribution to such a dynamic intellectualism.

7. *Op. cit.*, p.203.

8. Eph. 4.15.

9. Cf. D. Bonhoeffer, *Christ the Centre*, New York: Harper & Row (*Christology*, London: Collins) 1966, p.28.

10. St Augustine, *Confessions*, X, 24.

11. F. H. Bradley, *Appearance and Reality*, London: OUP 1893, p.5.

12. This chapter is based on an address given at a conference on spirituality at Trinity Institute, New York.

Chapter VII

1. Herbert Francis Smith, SJ, 'Truths and Half-truths about the Mass', *Eucharist*, September/October 1968.

2. *Understanding Media*, p.21.

3. This remark applies chiefly to the Roman communion, and, in a less degree, to the Anglican. The ministry of the Word has always been adequately represented in the Protestant churches. This will serve to remind us that all branches of Christendom do not have the same needs. What may be appropriate for Rome at this stage may not be appropriate for others, and should not be slavishly copied.

4. *Theology of Revelation*, p.127.

5. Gregory Dix, OSB. *The Shape of the Liturgy*, London: Dacre Press 1945, p.215.

6. F. L. Cross, *The Early Christian Fathers*, London: Duckworth 1960, p.167.

7. E. Schillebeeckx, *God and Man*, London: Sheed & Ward 1969, p.203.

8. A. M. Ramsey, *Sacred and Secular*, London: Longmans, and New York: Harper & Row 1965, p.57.

9. Allan D. Galloway, *Faith in a Changing Culture*, London: Allen & Unwin 1967; New York: Humanities Press 1968, pp.64f.

10. Hugh Ross Williamson, *The Great Prayer*, London: Collins 1955; New York: Macmillan 1956, p.173.

Chapter VIII

1. 'The faith of Easter is just this – faith in the word of preaching', *Kerygma and Myth*, ed. H.-W. Bartsch, London: SPCK 1953; New York: Macmillan 1954, p.41.

2. Ian Henderson, *Rudolph Bultmann*, London: Carey Kingsgate Press 1965; Richmond: John Knox Press 1966, p.47.

3. *Loc. cit.*

4. Hugh Montefiore, *Can Man Survive? 'The Question Mark' and other Essays*, rev. ed., London: Collins 1970, p.134.

5. Martin Buber, *I and Thou*, second ed., New York: Scribner 1958; Edinburgh: T. & T. Clark 1959, p.7f.

6. Joachim Jeremias, *The Eucharistic Words of Jesus*, revised ed., London: SCM Press, and New York: Scribner 1966, pp.220f.

7. I John 1.1.

8. See above, p. 80.

9. M. Heidegger, *Being and Time*, London: SCM Press, and New York: Harper and Row 1962, pp.91–148.

10. Joseph M. Powers, SJ, *Eucharistic Theology*, New York: Herder & Herder 1967: London; Burns Oates 1968, pp.138f.

11. See above, p.55.

12. This was changed to receptionist wording in the rite of 1552, but the original 'for us' has been restored in revisions of the Anglican rite, including the Church of England revision of 1967.

13. See above, p.74.

14. Justin, *Apology I*, 65.

15. The expression 'extra-liturgical' devotions is unfortunate. If it means devotions *in addition to* the eucharistic liturgy, it is acceptable: but if it means devotions *outisde of the liturgy*, it rests on a misunderstanding, for the devotions to which the expression refers are not outside the liturgy but extensions of it.

16. This chapter is based on an address given at the Second Liturgical Conference at the Church of St Mary the Virgin, New York.

Chapter IX

1. See above, Chapter VIII.

2. Walter Burkert, *Greek Religion*, Cambridge, Mass.: Harvard University Press 1985, p.66.

3. Denziger, 940.

4. Thomas Cranmer, *A Defence of the True and Catholic Doctrine of the Sacrament of the Body and Blood of our Saviour Christ*, Chas Thynne 1907, p.232.

5. Joachim Jeremias, *The Eucharistic Words of Jesus*, London: SCM Press and New York: Scribners 1969, pp.251–2.

6. *ARCIC Final Report*, London: SPCK 1982, pp.13–14.

7. G. Wainwright, *Eucharist and Eschatology*, London: Epworth Press 1971, p.67.

8. C. C. Richardson, 'Cranmer and the Analysis of Eucharistic Doctrine', *Journal of Theological Studies* XVI.2, 1965, p.421.

9. Jasper Ridley, *Thomas Cranmer*, London: OUP 1962, p.66.

10. Augustine, Sermon 272.

11. Quotations from the Archbishops' Letter are taken from the translation by E. R. Hardy in his pamphlet *Priesthood and Sacrifice in the English Church*, West Park, NY: Holy Cross Publications 1961.

12. *New English Hymnal* No.273. See also Canon Bright's hymn, *New English Hymnal* No.304.

Chapter X

1. Gen. 28.15.

2. Matt. 28.20.

3. *Confessions*, X, 35.

4. John 1.14.

5. William Temple, *Nature, Man and God*, London and New York: Macmillan 1934, p.478.

6. John 1.9.

7. Psalm 78.25.

8. John 6.51.

9. Hugh Blenkin, *Immortal Sacrifice*, London: Darton, Longman & Todd 1964, p.30.

10. Ps. 117.

11. Isa. 40.31.

Chapter XI

1. Ps. 119.164.

2. See above, p.19.

3. See above, p.5.

4. Evelyn Underhill, *Worship*, London: Nisbet, 1936; New York: Harper Bros. 1937, p.250.

5. D. Bonhoeffer, *Letters and Papers from Prison*, revised ed., London: SCM Press, and New York: Macmillan 1967, p.150.

6. See E. Bethge, *Dietrich Bonhoeffer*, pp.379, 778 etc.

7. See above, p.76.

8. See, for instance, the Church of England's 'Second Series' versions of 1967.

9. P. Drijvers, *The Psalms: their Structure and Meaning*, New York: Herder & Herder, and London: Burns & Oates 1965, p.7.

10. Ps. 139.21.

11. 'Psalms' in *The Jerome Biblical Commentary*, ed. Raymond E. Brown, Joseph A. Fitzmyer, Roland E. Murphy, London: Geoffrey Chapman 1970, vol. I, p.575.

12. Joseph P. Whelan, SJ, *The Spirituality of Friedrich von Hügel*, London: Collins 1971, p.18.

Chapter XII

1. James 1.23.

2. John Baillie, *The Sense of the Presence of God*, London: OUP, and New York: Scribner 1962, p.137.

3. Mark 8.34.

4. E. Troeltsch, 'Historiography', in *Contemporary Religious Thinkers*, ed. J. Macquarrie, London: SCM Press, and New York: Harper & Row 1968, p.88.

5. John 19.13.

6. Rom. 3.23.

7. See above, p.79.

8. Heb. 1.2.

9. Mark 15.21.

10. Mark 15.43.

11. Col. 1.24.

12. Michel Quoist, *Prayers of Life*, Dublin: Gill & Macmillan 1963, p.5.

13. Origen, *Contra Celsum*, VI, 79, tr. Henry Chadwick, London and New York: CUP 1953.

14. M. Luther, 'On the Liberty of the Christian Man', in *Works of Martin Luther*, Philadelphia: Muhlenberg Press 1943, vol. II, p.338.

Chapter XIII

1. Rudolf Bultmann, *History of the Synoptic Tradition*, Oxford: Blackwell and New York, Harper and Row 1968.

2. *The Shepherd of Hermas*, Commandment IV, Chapter 3.

3. Joseph Martos, *Doors to the Sacred*, New York: Doubleday and London: SCM Press 1981, p.325.

4. See Dietrich Bonhoeffer, *Life Together*, London: SCM Press and New York: Harper and Row 1954.

5. See John Kennedy, *Presbyterian Authority and Discipline*, Richmond, Va: John Knox Press 1965, Chapter 4.

6. For a specimen outline of service, entitled 'Communal Celebration of Penance and Peace', see Bernard Häring, *Shalom/Peace: The Sacrament of Reconciliation*, Garden City: Image Books 1969, p.301.

Chapter XIV

1. T. F. Torrance, *Theology in Reconciliation*, London: Geoffrey Chapman 1975, pp.277–8.

2. *The Hymnal 1940*, No.437.

3. A. M. Ramsey, *Sacred and Secular*, Longmans 1965, pp.52–3.

4. Eberhard Bethge, *Dietrich Bonhoeffer*, London: Collins and New York: Harper and Row 1970, pp.830–1.

5. Thomas Merton, *The Silent Life*, New York: Farrar, Straus and Cudahy 1957, p.150.

6. H. U. von Balthasar, *Elucidations*, London: SPCK 1975, p.119.

Chapter XV

1. See above, pp.7f.

2. Reinhold Niebuhr, *The Nature and Destiny of Man*, London: Nisbet, and New York: Scribner 1941–3, vol. I, p.21.

3. Schleiermacher's definition of 'true religion'. F. Schleiermacher, *On Religion*, New York: Harper & Row 1958, p.39.

4. Proinsias MacCana, *Celtic Mythology*, London: Hamlyn 1970, p.35.

5. Cf. G. R. D. McLean, *Poems of the Western Highlanders*, London: SPCK 1961.

6. R. G. Smith, *The Doctrine of God*, London: Collins, and Philadelphia: Westminster Press 1970, p.128.

7. His teaching is to be found chiefly in *Our Knowledge of God*, London, OUP, and New York: Scribner 1939, and in *The Sense of the Presence of God*: London: OUP, and New York: Scribner 1962.

8. *Prayers of Life*, p. iii.

9. *Le Milieu Divin*, pp.38, 56.

10. *Ibid.*, p.115.

Index of Names

Addison, Joseph, 162
Alves, Rubem, 3, 160
Augustine of Hippo, St, 7, 101, 109, 163, 164

Baillie, John, 124, 157, 165
Balthasar, H. U. von, 150, 166
Barth, Karl, 57–8, 147
Bartsch, H.-W., 163
Benedict, St, 17
Bethge, Eberhard, 161, 165, 166
Blenkin, Hugh, 113, 165
Bonhoeffer, Dietrich, 24, 39, 57–8, 118, 136, 148–9, 161, 163, 165, 166
Braaten, Carl, 2
Bradley, F. H., 72, 163
Bright, William, 105, 164
Brigid, St, 156
Brown, Raymond E., 165
Buber, Martin, 163
Buddha, Buddhism, 27, 39
Bultmann, Rudolf, 57–8, 84, 133, 166
Burkert, Walter, 164

Calvin, John, Calvinism, 155
Celsus, 130
Chadwick, Henry, 166
Columba, St, 125
Cone, James H., 160
Cox, Harvey, 3
Cranmer, Thomas, 81, 91, 95, 99–100, 119, 121
Cross, F. L., 78, 163
Cyril of Alexandria, St, 47

Damien, Father, 28
Diekman, Godfrey, 14
Dix, Gregory, 76, 78, 97, 100, 163
Drijvers, Pius, 120, 165

Eckhardt, John, 34, 161

Eichrodt, Walther, 41, 162
Eliade, Mircea, 7

Felici, Louis, 109, 113
Feuerbach, Ludwig, 4, 7, 56–7, 160
Fitzmyer, J. A., 165
Freud, Sigmund, 4

Galloway, Allan D., 80, 163
Gibbard, Mark, 38, 77, 161
Gregory of Nyssa, 145

Hammarskjöld, Dag, 24, 32, 34, 161
Hardy, E. R., 164
Häring, Bernard, 38, 161, 166
Haushofer, Albrecht, 39, 161
Hegel, G. W. F., 41, 96, 162
Heidegger, Martin, 89, 164
Henderson, Ian, 84, 163
Heurtley, C. A., 162
Hippolytus, 78
Husserl, Edmund, 71

Irenaeus, St, 15, 161

Jaspers, Karl, 37, 54, 161
Jeremias, Joachim, 86, 99, 164
Johnson, Samuel, 125
Joseph of Arimathea, St, 129
Justin, St, 92, 164

Leo XIII, Pope, 103
Luther, Martin, 7, 130, 166

MacCana, Proinsias, 166
Maclagan, William, 103
McLean, G. R. D., 166
McLuhan, Marshall, 32, 37, 59, 74–5, 161
Marcel, Gabriel, 31
Martos, Joseph, 166
Marx, Karl, 4